Rhonda C Douglas
Tel: (281) 379-4250

Alastair Sawday's
Special Places to Stay

Italy

1st Edition

Edited by Susan Pennington

Typesetting, Conversion & Repro:	Avonset, Bath
Maps:	Bartholomew Mapping Services, a division of HarperCollins Publishers, Glasgow
Printing:	Midas Book Printers UK
Design:	Caroline King & Springboard Design, Bristol
UK Distribution:	Portfolio, London
US Distribution:	The Globe Pequot Press, Guilford, Connecticut

First published in March 2000 by:
Alastair Sawday Publishing Co. Ltd
44 Ambra Vale East, Bristol BS8 4RE, UK.

The Globe Pequot Press
P.O. Box 480
Guilford, Connecticut
06437
USA

First edition 2000

ISBN 1-901970-09-4 Printed in Slovenia

ISBN 0-7627-0721-6 Printed in US

Alastair Sawday's
Special Places to Stay

Italy

"Italy is my magnet."

Lord Byron

The
Globe
Pequot
Press

Guilford
Connecticut, USA

ASP

Alastair Sawday Publishing
Bristol, UK

Acknowledgements

An editor needs to know how to navigate through the tangled thickets of laws, customs, preconceived ideas, rejections, evasions and irregularities. And that is not to mention the equally impressive tangle of wines, aperitifs, pastas and delights that make up Italian hospitality. (And can you imagine what impact the word 'inspector' has on an Italian householder/business-person?)

So, a sense of humour is put to daily use. Above all Susan Pennington has displayed doggedness and enthusiasm in equal measure, unearthing some remarkable places and people in a country much of which is over-run with hotels and tourists, and much is little visited. It isn't easy, when so many hundreds of gorgeous places have been ruined by bad taste. The challenge has been considerable.

Others have toiled valiantly: the ineffable Jayne Warren started us off and Lucinda Carling penetrated the most obscure corners of Italy, all with the greatest of good humour. We will never know how much Massimo, Susan's partner, has had to put up with. Julia Richardson has fended off the army of problems that stop a book getting to a fit state to be printed. Russell Wilkinson has been another vital mechanic, wielding tools hitherto unknown to us. Annie Shillito rescued the book from me when she took over as Managing Editor and has gathered it into shape with humour and skill.

Lastly, Bob Wilson has typeset the book with his usual intelligence and perseverance. He deserves medals, not least because we continually invented new spanners to throw into his works.

Alastair Sawday

Series Editor:	Alastair Sawday
Editor:	Susan Pennington
Managing Editor:	Annie Shillito
Production Manager:	Julia Richardson
Additional writers:	Lindsay Butler; Lindsay Hunt, Celia Skrine
Administration:	Kate Harris, Russell Wilkinson
Inspections:	John Bolton, Lucinda Carling, Frances Cooper, Carolyn McKenzie, Jenny Shaw, Sarah Stevenson
Accounts:	Sheila Clifton, Sandra Hasell, Maureen Humphries
PR/Marketing:	Jayne Warren
Cover design:	Caroline King
Title page photographs:	Sarah Carson, Sara Hay, Jenny Shaw E.N.I.T. Roma

Thanks to Massimo Donati & Milo Tronconi in Italy for their help and everyone in Bristol for their eternal patience and support. *Susan*

Introduction

We have been pressed and cajoled to do this book for years. People have expressed their astonishment at our idiocy in not having done it already.

It's true that Italy is too ravishingly lovely for us NOT to do a *Special Places* guide on it. So, Susan has pressed ahead and discovered over a hundred of those places for which these books have become famous: interesting, highly individual, owned by delightful people and often in stunning areas. The collection within these pages is as eclectic as any we have published - beautiful villas, simple farmhouses, tiny hotels and magnificent old ladies in stone. They should bring relief to all of you who have longed to travel to Italy in our sort of style, choosing between the sybaritic and the simple, the coolly professional and the engagingly amateur... using our carefully chosen words to guide you away from the place that would be wrong for you. On Saturday you may feel like whooping it up in Rome; on Sunday you may need to bury your aching head in the hills. We've thought of it all.

This is an exciting beginning to our Italy project. We ask owners to pay to feature in the book, and it takes time to build up the trust that we have earned in other countries. The next edition will have an even richer selection of special places for you. Do let us know of places for which you have a particular affection.

Alastair Sawday

Introduction

The Writing

It is dauntingly difficult to avoid cliché and hyberbole, and we have no doubt fallen into every trap... but only occasionally, I hope. The inevitable repetitive expression of surprise, admiration and delight has to be couched in a hundred different ways. Above all we must tell the truth, for if there is a funny little place up a back street in some obscure town you will want to know why we have included it, and whether you - with that particular friend - should avoid it. We try hard to distinguish between the sort of place to which a 50-year-old executive would want to take his wife in order to impress her, and the places where you might want to take your unruly family.

Note that we never let the owners do their own writing; the results would usually be disastrous, however many hundreds of hours we would save. They always want to tell you how 'welcoming' they are (understandably) and how many bits of equipment they have in the bedrooms, as if you were bound to be a frustrated technophile.

Ratings

These are often the products of bureaucratic minds which attach priority to non-essentials like room-size and elevators, though - to be fair - it is no bad thing to have an official rating system as a general guide. Our own criteria are so different that we avoid mention of ratings and studiously avoid creating a system of our own. We try to use words and photographs instead because, above all, we value such elusive qualities as genuine personal charm, historical authenticity, character, beauty and peace... and a bit of fun.

How do we choose?

We try to avoid the ugly, the banal, the aloof and the over-priced. So you have in your hands a selection of places that our team of inspired inspectors consider *special* at whatever price. There are no hard and fast rules; the important thing is that we should want to stay there ourselves. We show you a wonderful array of really special places to stay, ranging from *agriturismo* farms to four-star hotels. Each place will give you more than a mere taste of Italy and Italian hospitality, and is here primarily because we LIKE it. There is no history of bed and breakfast as there is in Britain; the Italian breakfast of a diminutive cup of coffee quickly slugged back with a sweet pastry hardly makes for a satisfying meal, but this isn't what it's all about. Italy is abnormally rich in culture and traditions, and of course great food and wine, and we're showing you how to get under its skin. We have largely avoided hotels in the big towns and cities, though Rome is the exception. Instead we have opted for smaller properties within easy reach of famous places, so you can make day trips by car or use public transport.

THINGS YOU SHOULD KNOW

Regional variations - Each region of Italy differs hugely from the next. The famous Italian bureaucracy is part of the reason; the laws are different in each region, making it difficult to have general classifications. For example, the standard of an *agriturismo* in Tuscany is much higher than in Emilia

Introduction

Romagna. However you will probably get more genuine hospitality and home cooking in Parma than in Siena. On the coast the emphasis in on the outdoors and of course, for many folk, those old stone floors and wonky walls we dearly love were a reminder of hardship and poverty, and many have been replaced by characterless tiles and smooth finishes.

Types of accommodation

In the index the type of propety (e.g Podere, Hotel) is listed after the proper name.

Agriturismo	Farm with rooms or apartments. You will come across other associated terms such as *Azienda Agraria* (*Az. Ag*) - farm company.
Albergo	The Italian word for 'hotel' but generally smaller and a little more personal that its larger sister.
Ca' or Casa	House.
Cascina/Podere	Originally a farmhouse.
Corte	Country villa.
Locanda/Relais	Literally meaning 'inn', but often sometimes used to describe a restaurant only.
Palazzo	Not necessarily a palace but a large building.
Apartments	Many of the places in this book have rooms and apartments, some only apartments. They are generally self-catering and usually let by the week. See listing at back of book.

Room coding and prices

S = Single, D = Double, Tw = Twin, Tr = Triple, Q = Quadruple, Ste = Suite, Apt = Apartment

'en suite' indicates that the room has its own bath/shower + w.c.

Where room prices given are 'per person', rather than per room, they are followed by 'p.p.' Prices include tax.

Where a single price is given and no single rooms are shown, that price refers to single occupancy of a double/twin room.

Meal prices are per person.

Voltage and energy - Italy runs on 220V, with the rest of Europe; however you will need an adaptor as sockets are two or three pin. Pick one up before you leave or at the airport as they are not easy to find. Convertors work well for shavers and radios but make a hairdryer rather pathetic (most places will be happy to lend you one). Power surges and cuts are frequent, particularly in the country; the standard is 3kW for each house so there are few electrical appliances such as dryers, microwaves, kettles etc. Electricity in Italy is precious and more expensive than water so please remember to turn off lights to be considerate to your hosts.

Introduction

Bathrooms tend to go from one extreme to the other, from the wildly extravagant with marble flooring and crystal fixtures to shoe boxes with an open shower between the bidet and the w.c. The majority in this book are entirely adequate; showers are the norm, or there may be a small bath, with a bidet and w.c. in the same room. As long as your expectations are reasonable you should get no unpleasant surprises.

Towels are usually supplied but are rarely the large fluffy ones. Many are the very Italian cotton sheet type or the honeycombed textured ones. Face flannels (wash cloths) are considered very personal and so are not provided.

Beds vary greatly in size; some of the singles really are narrow but, in contrast, the doubles are usually queen-size. In many twin rooms beds can be pushed together and often you can ask for an extra bed.

General décor - Italians tend to throw little away and are very adept at mixing and matching. Don't be surprised if you find, say, a handsome 18th-century chest next to a very nondescript bedside table. Carpets and rugs are unusual, so stone, marble and terracotta floors are often bare, which can be a rude awakening. A good tip is to take slippers or buy a pair of 'polishing' slippers which you can find with the cleaning goods in the supermarket or hardware store for only L2,000.

Banks

Opening hours are between 8.20am and 1.20pm. In rural areas banks don't always open in the afternoon but in the larger towns and cities they do, between 2.30pm and 3.30pm. Most banks have outside ATMs or cashpoints which will accept most cards.

The Italian lire can be confusing with all those '0's' - some people think they've suddenly become rich! You will also now, of course, see prices in Euros and we've included a conversion table at the back of this guide.

Methods of Payment

Credit Cards are now fairly widely accepted, but do check, particularly with the smaller places.
Travellers cheques are generally not welcome.
Eurocheques are more readily accepted as they can be written in the local currency.

Using the Telephone

The country code for Italy is 00 39. The city or town code is three or four digits starting with '0' and you need to use this even when calling from within the district. (The usual reply is *pronto*, which literally means 'ready'.)

Telephoning in Italy is no longer expensive. Italian telephone cards are widely available, at L5,000 and L10,000 and very convenient - remember to break off the perforated corner! Long distance phone (calling) cards, can also be used cheaply; don't use them for local calls or calls within Europe.

Introduction

Children

There can be few better places than Italy to bring children; all but the smartest of hotels and restaurants welcome them with open arms. We have given a 'child' symbol for places we think are particularly child-friendly.

Dogs and cats

The dog symbol shows where they are welcome - but do double-check this when booking. The cat symbol shows where the owners have animals of their own.

A word of warning - On rural properties dogs and cats are generally kept not so much as pets but as working animals. Usually they live outside; dogs are often kept on chains and the cats you see wandering around may look lost and forlorn - don't succumb to those pleading eyes. It's common too, on the outskirts of villages, to find groups of hunting dogs kept together. You often hear them barking at night, disturbed by wildlife. It's all part of the way of life. Apart from guide dogs, animals are legally barred from restaurants.

Registration

Guests have to be registered with the police within 24 hours of their arrival. This applies not just to foreigners but to anyone who is not a resident of the district.

The police - receipts

As you travel around you will see the different branches of the Italian police force at the roadside carrying out routine checks. You may need to prove your identity so always carry your passport. It's also not unusual for the police to be armed with rather alarming machine guns. Another oddity: it is important to keep your receipts from shops or restaurants as there are special police checks for this too.

Making a booking

It is best to make your booking in writing; at the back of this book is a sample form. Often you will need to pay a deposit of the equivalent of one night's stay or 30% of a week's holiday. You can do this by credit card, personal cheque or bank transfer. Do make sure that you have written confirmation and ask for detailed directions. It's best to check and get more details than we have space for here.

Check-in/out times

Check-in is generally after 2pm for hotels (check-out by midday) and for apartments and B&Bs check-in is after 4pm (check-out by 10am). If you are going to be late, let owners know... they might give your room away to someone else.

Driving

For some the mere thought of driving in Italy sends the heart racing. However - and although we're keen to encourage exploration on foot, bike and public transport - for some it's the only way they can explore. If you're not taking your own car it's usually cheaper, and more reliable, to organise car rental from your own country.

Introduction

Maps - Make sure you have a decent map. If you are planning to spend some time in a particular region it's worth investing in a local one. Be aware that map symbols can differ between publishers and that roads may not be numbered or may be numbered slightly differently from the signposts(!). The following are general guidelines (the size and condition of the road can vary within each category).

Autostrada - Toll motorways, usually with 4 lanes. Indicated with green signs and numbers preceded by 'A'. Generally shown on maps with a bold double black line. Make sure you take the toll ticket. If you don't you will be charged for the entire stretch of the motorway.

Superstrada - Primary routes usually shown in bold red and similar to an Autostrada but without the tolls. Marked 'SS' or 'ss'.

Strada Statale - State roads, usually in finer red and also marked 'SS' or 'ss'.

Strada Provincial - Secondary routes, marked in yellow and with numbers preceded by 'prov'. Often very windy. Marked 'SP' or 'sp'.

Strada Bianca - Unpaved roads that often have no number at all. These are generally very quiet and often lead through lovely countryside, but it's easy to get lost.

Fuel - Petrol is more expensive in Italy than in the UK and much more expensive than in the USA. Don't wait until you hit red on the gauge before filling up as you can often go for many miles (even on the biggest roads) without coming across a station. You have been warned!

Some key words

Super - Regular petrol
Verde/senza piombo - Unleaded petrol
Gas olio/diesel - Diesel
Pieno per favore - A full tank please

Self-service in Italy until recently meant getting petrol when the station was closed. Insert either a L10,000 or L50,000 note in the machine, select the pump number, go to that pump, and fill up the car. You can also use a credit card but many machines have a nasty habit of being stubborn about taking the card. Recently the larger companies have taken the plunge and now offer self-service during opening hours, with a special discount if you serve yourself as there are still attendants there to help.

Public transport is good and reliable, but do check times as it's frustrating, if you have a shopping spree in mind, to arrive somewhere at midday just as everything is shutting down for lunch (followed, of course, by siesta).

Public Holidays
Be warned that on the day before a public holiday - and there are a lot of them in Italy - Italians rush out to buy everything in sight. Check-out queues are long. *Ferragosto* is probably the most important; it marks the summer holiday for Italians and for the following two weeks many places totally close down and whole families and even large companies take a holiday. This is particularly felt in the cities. Although shops etc are closed, many restaurants are not, so don't worry about starving.

Introduction

January 1	New Year's Day	Capo d'anno
January 6	Epiphany	La Befana
Late March/April	Easter	Pasqua
April 25	Liberation Day	Venticinque aprile
May 1	Labour Day	Primo Maggio
August 15	Assumption of the Virgin	Ferragosto
November 1	All Saints, Day	Tutti Santi
December 8	Feast of the Immaculate Conception	Festa dell' Immacolata
December 25	Christmas Day	Natale
December 26	Boxing Day	Santo Stefano

There are also lots of other pagan holidays all over Italy and each town has its patron saint who, of course, has his/her holiday too. There are also local fetes and holidays which you shouldn't miss out on. Italians are wonderful dancers and it's refreshing to see grand-parents, parents, children and sometimes even a fourth generation, all dancing together.

Eating in Italy

Do be brave. There are so many good cooks hidden within the pages of this book that you will miss out if you don't plunge in and eat everything you are offered. Each region has its specialities and eating in Italy can be every bit as entertaining as doing so in France.

Breakfast - What constitutes breakfast varies from place to place. Italians generally grab a cappuccino or a strong black coffee with loads of sugar in a tiny cup, and a sweet pastry in the bar on the way to work. On the farms you should find something a little more substantial like fruit juice and home-made jam and bread, though you might have to ask for butter. Hotels may lay on the universal 'continental buffet' which often includes cold meats, cheeses, yoghurt and cereal. (Take your own tea-bags if you're fussy!)

Evening meals - Many of the properties do offer evening meals but often you need to let them know well in advance if you'd like to eat in.

In Italy it is not usual to eat with your host families. Normally there is a separate dining room for guests and a member of the family will wait on you; there is enough confusion in the kitchen with the family!

A jug of house wine might cost L5,000 whereas a bottle of it might be L10,000 and a bottle from the wine list L50,000. There is no need to work your way through all four or five courses; it is quite acceptable to have *antipasti* and *secondi* (starter and a main dish) or other combinations. Ordering *cappuccino* after a meal is somewhat frowned upon as it's thought of as a breakfast drink; but Italians are getting used to our strange eating habits! Pizza is not generally available for lunch, apart from in the fast food places which are beginning to rear their ugly heads in Italy too.

Vegetarians should not have too many problems, though it is rare to find 'veggie' main courses. You may baffle the waiter by asking specifically for them, but between the starters, pasta and side dishes there is plenty of choice.

Produce is usually fresh and seasonal; if something has been frozen there is usually an asterisk next to that item on the menu.

Introduction

Timing is important - Restaurants outside cities are generally not open all day. Lunch is served between 12 noon and 2.30pm and even at 2.30pm you might get rather a cool reception. Supper is from 7.30pm - 10.00pm; as many restaurants are family-run you will find them all sitting in the kitchen any earlier, having their own supper.

Children. Many restaurants have high chairs and most are willing to modify dishes for children producing, say, a plate of plain pasta with butter and cheese. Of course this means other people's children are hard to avoid, whether at midday or in the evening.

Tipping. You will usually find *coperto* at the top of the bill; this is a cover charge which ranges from L2,500 - L8,000 lire per person. This is for the use of the table, linen, cutlery and bread. Only in the larger or city restaurants, or possibly if you are with a large group, is service automatically added to your bill, so in the smaller or off-the-beaten-track places you can leave a tip if you wish.

The concept of a 'doggy bag' does not really exist in Italy and where it is understood it is actually rather looked down upon as giving the impression of being mean or cheap... *la bella figura*!

www.sawdays.co.uk
You can access more than 700 Special Places in Britain, France, Spain, Portugal and Ireland at this address and the site is growing.

Special Places Travel Club
With nearly 2,500 Special Places in seven countries we are in a wonderful position to offer our readers something special. This Travel Club brings together our keenest readers to give them big discounts on books, special deals on our Special Places Walks (see back of book for advert) and other offers as they arise. Let us know if you are interested.

Finally
Your comments are always welcome and vital to us. There is a report form at the back of the book. If you know and love a place that we have not included, please tell us. If your recommendation is included in one of our books you will be sent a free copy of the next edition.

Ideas on how we can improve our books are also extremely helpful. After all, they are for you.

Very finally
Have a wonderful time in Italy.

Symbols

Explanations of symbols - treat each one as a guide rather than as a statement of fact.

 Working farm.

 Fairly to very good English is spoken here.

 Children are welcomed but cots, high chairs etc are not necessarily available. The text gives restrictions where relevant.

 You can either borrow or hire bikes here.

 Good hiking walks from house or village.

 Some, but not all, ingredients are organically grown.

 Vegetarians catered for with advance warning.

 Full disabled facilities provided.

 Pets are welcome but may be housed in an outbuilding rather than in your room. Check when booking if restrictions apply.

 This house has pets of its own: dog, cat, horse, duck, parrot.

 Applies to totally non-smoking houses.

 Swimming nearby - a pond, a lake, a river or the sea.

 Credit cards are accepted.

Disclaimer

We make no claims to pure objectivity in judging our Special Places to Stay. They are here because we like them. Our opinions and tastes are ours alone and this book is a statement of them; we cross our fingers and hope that you will share them.

We have done our utmost to get our facts right but apologise unreservedly for any mistakes that may have crept in. Sometimes, too, prices shift, usually upward, and 'things' change. We would be grateful to be told of any errors or changes, however small.

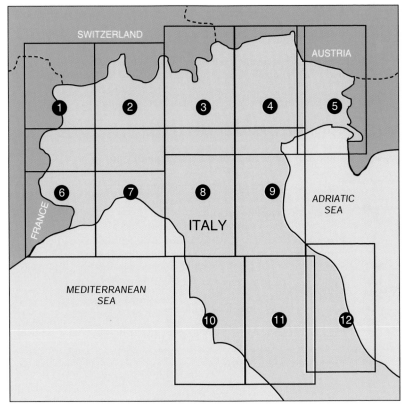

General Map

Contents

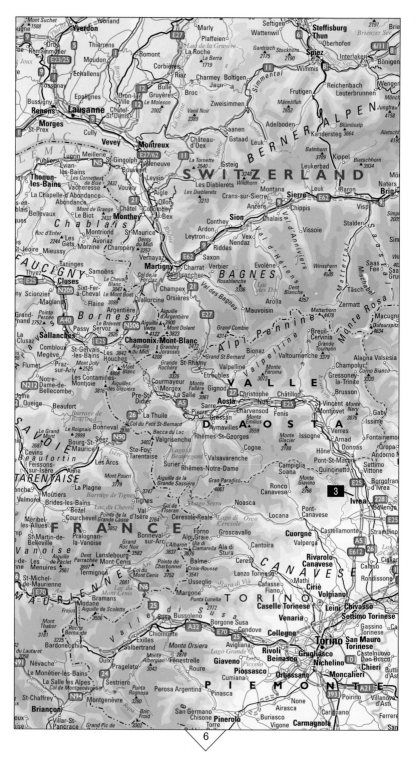

1   **Scale for colour maps** 1:1M

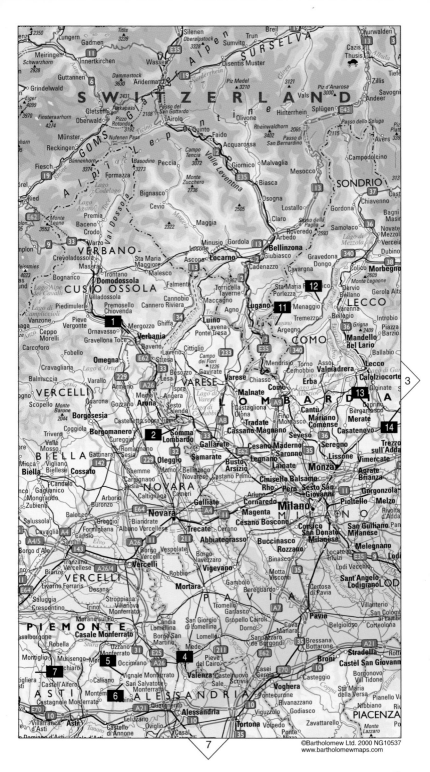

©Bartholomew Ltd. 2000 NG10537
www.bartholomewmaps.com

2

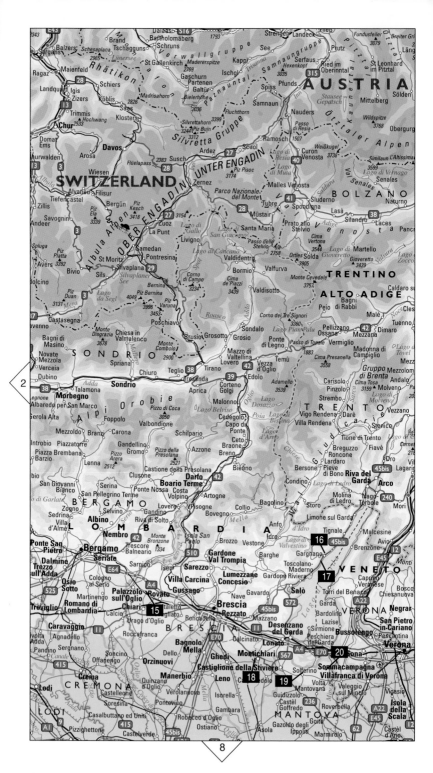

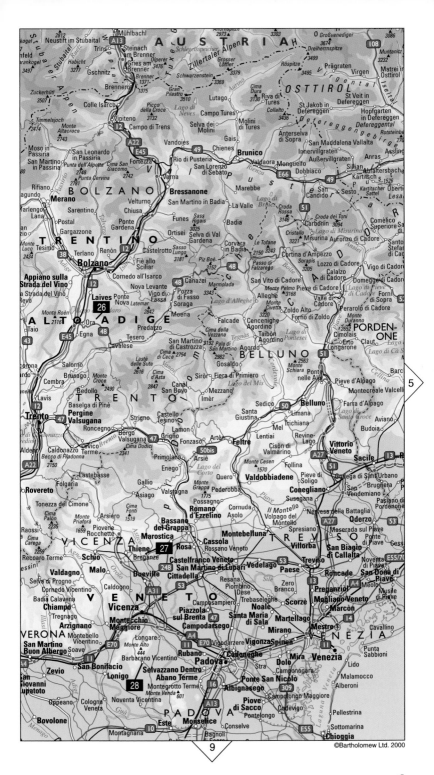

4

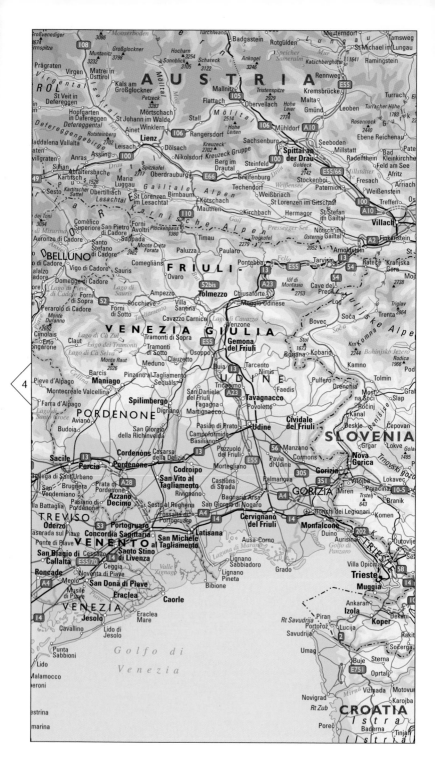

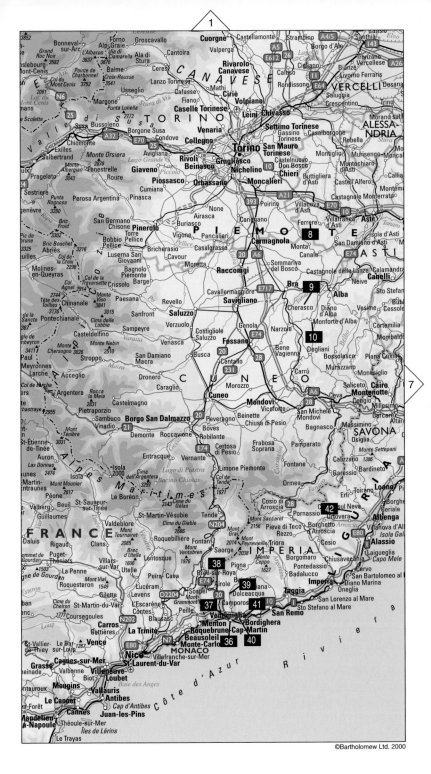

6

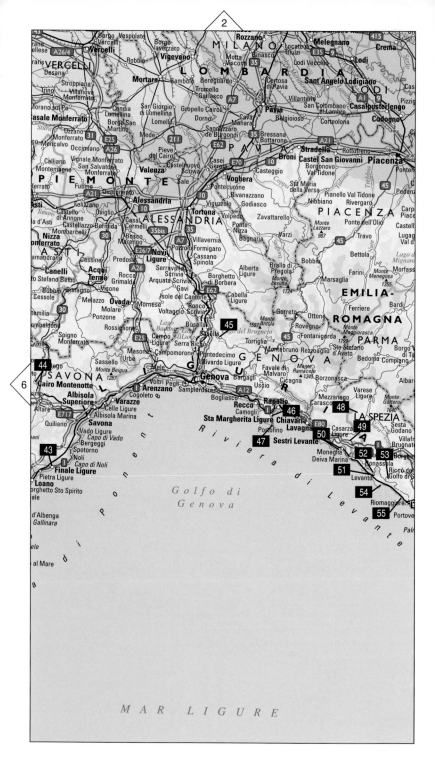

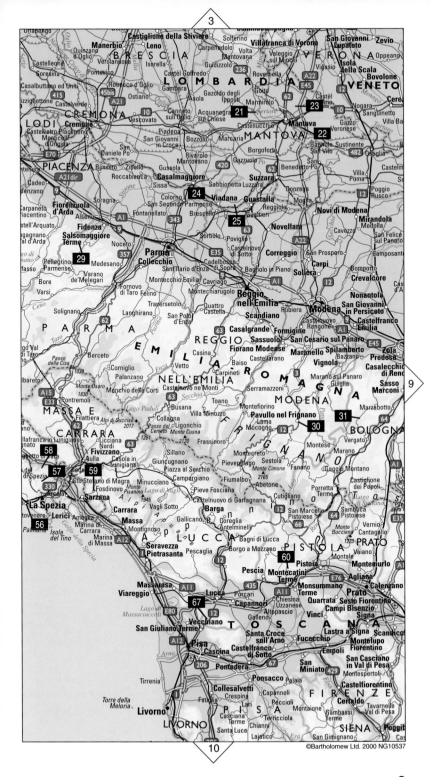

8

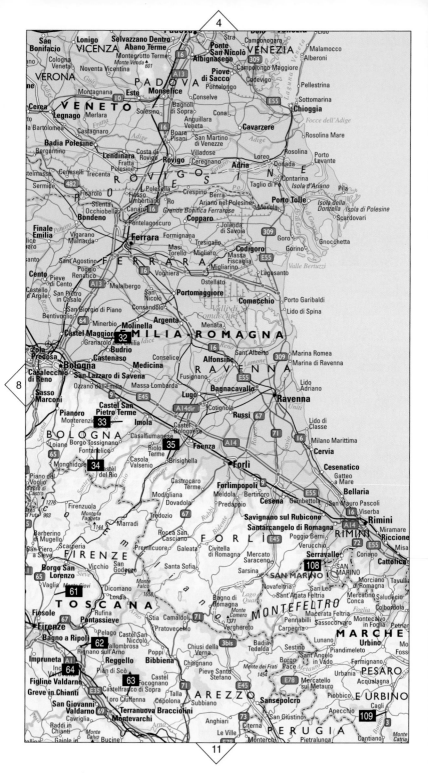

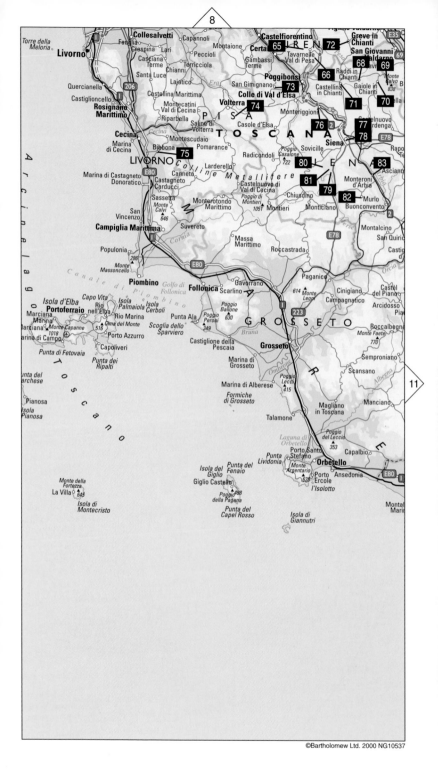

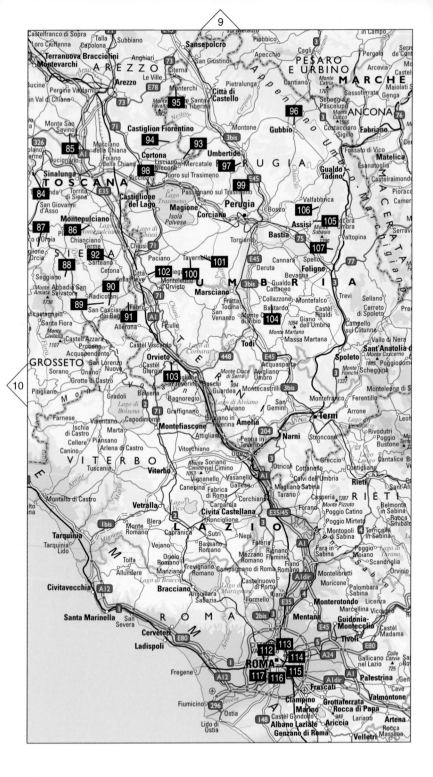

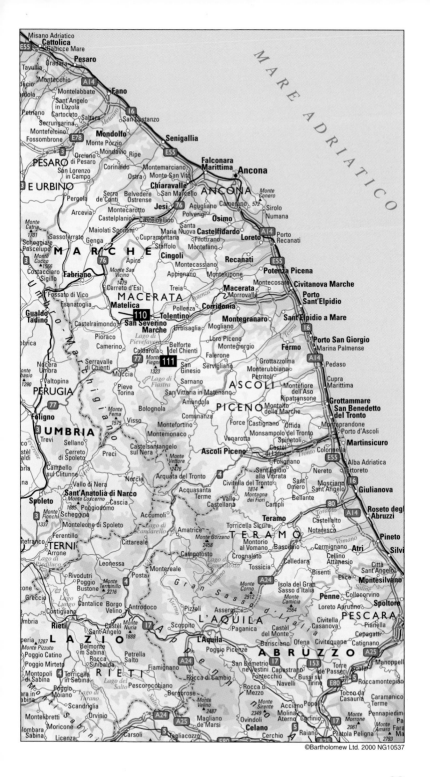

Piedmont

"Everything you see I owe to spaghetti."
Sophia Loren

Le Oche di Bracchio

Via Bracchio 46
28040 Mergozzo NO

Tel: 0323 801 22
Fax: 0323 806 92
E-mail: hatga@tin.it

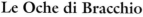

Sig.ra Alessandra Galbiasi

Church bells are likely to be one of the few sounds you'll hear. Mergozzo is a small and pretty town on the shores of one of Italy's least polluted lakes. Le Oche di Bracchio is on the outskirts, in a peaceful setting, though its lake views are rather obscured by trees. It's a neat, cheerful and typically Italian place, with a modern hotel of convenient if unexceptional rooms. Across the orchard, though, is something more unusual — a converted 19th-century *collegio* used as an annexe and containing several large self-catering units. Furnishings are mostly functional rather than old or charming, but the warm welcome of the delightful Alessandra more than makes up for any lack of decorative imagination. The other great plus point of this place is its restaurant. Sra Galbiati loves cooking and the regional menus offer plenty of choice at each course. An even more surprising feature of the hotel is its two large studio gyms used by arts groups as dance and drama workshops, and for hatha yoga sessions taught by Alessandra's husband. A spot of shiatsu massage or a bake in the sauna may soothe away any travel tension.

Rooms: 16: 1 S, 8 D, 6 Tr, 1 Q, all en suite.
Price: S L90,000-100,000; D L160,000-180,000; Tr L100,000-120,000.
Breakfast: Included.
Meals: Lunch L30,000; Dinner L50,000.
Closed: 5 January-5 February.

How to get there: Exit A26 at Gravellona Toce and follow directions for Verbania and Mergozzo. At traffic lights in Mergozzo turn left and continue for a further 1km.

Map Ref No: 2

Cascina Cesarina
Via dei Cesari 32
28040 Borgo Ticino NO

Tel: 0321 904 91

Sig.ra Clare Buckley

Clare is English but has lived in Italy since she was a teenager and her husband is Italian. This is not tourist country and almost all the guests at the farm are Italian, though an Englishness, of course, remains: main courses are strictly Italian home-cooking but you will recognise the puddings. Locals find the bathrooms very 'English' but you may not notice this. Unusually, at Cascina Cesarina you really will be living with the family, which includes a couple of bilingual teenagers. You will be eating with them in a large farmhouse kitchen and joining them afterwards to read or watch television. Clare is happy to cook lunch or dinner and uses all her own or local organic produce. The bedrooms are simple, with white walls, sandblasted wooden ceilings and country furniture. They look either onto the farmyard or onto a charming, rather dishevelled garden which runs into a nature reserve. If you prefer camping, Clare will find you a great spot. The farm is quite remote, ideal for long walks with the comforting thought of a cool pool waiting for you at the house.

Rooms: 2 D, both en suite.
Price: S L58,000; D L106,000.
Breakfast: Included.
Meals: Lunch on request L27,000;
Dinner L27,000.
Closed: Christmas & New Year.

How to get there: On the A26 m'way exit at Castelletto Ticovo, follow SS336 to Novara until you reach Borgo Ticino. There, turn right at the school. After 0.5km take the left fork for Gagnano, follow road down and under the arch on the left, straight into the farmyard and on to Cascina Cesarina.

Map Ref No: 2

La Miniera
Via delle Miniere 9
10010 Calea di Lessolo TO

Tel: 0125 586 18
Fax: 0125 561 963
E-mail: robyanau@tin.it

Sig.ra Roberta Anau

The former headquarters of a disused iron-ore mine in 40 acres of woodland was completely derelict when Roberta Anau and her husband bought it. It has now, we promise you, been transformed. The Anaus live in the former mine office with their large collection of dogs; the manager's house has been converted into simple guestrooms, while a smaller house in the garden has some better equipped self-catering places. In yet another building, the owners are steadily assembling a museum on the history of the mine, which dates from Roman times. Plus points include the large, lush garden which has been established with surprising success on top of the old mine spoil, and Roberta's interesting Jewish-Italian cooking; wild fungi and berries picked from the woods above the house find their way into her seasonal menus. There are shady terraces, ruins to explore and even Napoleonic mule tracks. Lovers of wildlife may spot some of the local owls that live in the woods nearby and wild boar may wander round the garden from time to time — Roberta doesn't seems to mind in the slightest. An unusual and rewarding place.

Rooms: 4 + 2 Apts: 4 D, all en suite;
2 Apt for 3-4.
Price: D L80,000-90,000; Apt L130,000.
Breakfast: L5000.
Meals: Weekends only L40,000-45,000 on request.
Closed: Never, restaurant closed January and second half of August.

How to get there: From Ivrea follow signs to Lessolo for 6km. Ignore first sign for Lessolo, continuing for a further 1.5km, then turn left towards Calea. Follow signs for La Miniera to the green iron gates.

Map Ref No: 1

Cascina Nuova
Strada per Pavia 2
15048 Valenza AL

Tel: 0131 954 763
Fax: 0131 928 553

Sig.ra Armanda Felli

Cascina Nuova would not suit everyone. Federico, who is friendly and sociable when he has time, farms 300 acres of corn, sunflowers and poplar trees and has nearly achieved his goal of becoming fully organic. It's a real farm, with tractors parked all over the place, so don't expect 'pretty pretty'. The apartments are in an old stable block but don't look very rustic. Two are on the ground floor and have been specially designed for wheelchair users. The other five are reached by a large communal terrace looking over the farmyard. The rooms are big but modern: you will not feel you are in a farmhouse. Breakfast is over at the main house, in a special room. It's good, with plenty of Federico's own produce; his equally friendly wife, Armanda, is busy on the farm and can only cook breakfast. You can buy eggs, vegetables, jam and home-made bread from this cornucopia, however. The region is not big on tourism but this is a good spot for a short break on your way further south. Hikers and bikers will find plenty to do, while Federico will show you where to fish or ride.

Rooms: 5 Apt.
Price: S L90,000; D L100,000; TR/Q L120,000 per night.
Breakfast: Self-catering. Breakfast available on request L10,000.
Meals: Self-catering.
Closed: Never.

How to get there: From Valenza follow signs to Milano, Casale, Pavia. The farm is on the right 1km out of town.

Map Ref No: 2

Il Mongetto Dre' Caste'

Via Piave 2
15049 Vignale Monferrato AL

Tel: 0142 933 442
Fax: 0142 933 469
E-mail: mongetto@italnet.it
web: www.mongetto.it

Sig. Carlo Santopietro

Il Mongetto shows you two sides of Italian life. Once you find it, hidden behind a high wall, through an imposing archway, you will be in a handsome 18th-century townhouse. Your home-made jam at breakfast, however, will come from the farm a couple of miles away. Carlo, too, is something of a contradiction: urbane, with a sly sense of humour, he produces wine, fruit and vegetables on his organic farm but does not preach about it, as some green enthusiasts do. The huge double rooms have frescoed ceilings and antique country furniture. The best find, however, are the two top-floor apartments, where wood is left dry and chopped for you to burn in the open fireplaces. You can have breakfast outside on a terrace, as early or as late as the mood takes you. Staff can come to cook you dinner on Friday and Saturday nights and Sunday lunchtime, using produce from the farm. One warning: as the rice fields of Vercelli are not too far away, you may need to take mosquito cream if the little beasts usually find you irresistible.

Rooms: 3 + 2 Apt: 1 D with en suite bathroom, 2 D sharing bathroom, 2 Apt for 2.
Price: D L90,000-100,000.
Breakfast: L10,000.
Meals: Dinner L40,000 Friday & Saturday; Lunch L40,000 Sunday.
Closed: Christmas, January, 15-31 August.

How to get there: In Vignale, continue through Piazza Mezzarda towards Camagna. At approx. 200m on the right is a very large archway with (usually closed) wooden doors. These are very easily missed, but are the entrance.

Cascina Alberta

Loc. Ca' Prano 14
15049 Vignale Monferrato AL

Tel: 0142 933 313
Fax: 0142 933 313

Sig.ra Raffaella De Cristofaro

People rave about this attractive hilltop farmhouse in the heart of a famous wine-producing area and you will, too. The house is two kilometres from the town centre in complete peace, marked by two stately cypress trees and with panoramic 360-degree views of the surrounding vineyards and the Monferrato hills beyond. The business is run on agriturismo lines. Guest bedrooms are extremely pretty with beds painted duck egg blue, walls soft pastel colours and each is carefully furnished with well-chosen pieces. The bedrooms and the prettily frescoed dining room are across the farmyard from the main house. Good regional cooking at very reasonable prices is an added bonus, with own-label wines from the estate — these include the DOC Barbera D'Asti and Grignolino del Monferrato Casalese, some of which are aged in wooden barrels and are hard to find outside the area. Raffaella pours huge amounts of energy and love into her cascina — she speaks excellent English and is happy to help guests get the most out of this enchanting area. Monferrato is about an hour's drive from the coast.

Rooms: 3 D, all en suite. Extra bed can be provided.
Price: S L50,000; D L90,000.
Breakfast: Included.
Meals: Lunch L25,000.
Closed: January and 15 days in summer.

How to get there: Go to Vignale to the corner piazza and follow the signs to Camagna. After 2km on the left there is a tiny roadside chapel, turn left and Cascina Alberta is after 400 metres on the right.

6

Cascina Piola

Via Fontana 2
Fraz. Serra
14014 Capriglio AT

Tel: 0141 997 447
Fax: 0141 997 447

Sig.ra Raffaella Firpo

Raffaella and Piero are former teachers who left Turin 15 years ago to bring up their two children in the country. With the produce from their organic smallholding, they make and sell large quantities of jam and preserves. Cascina Piola is a late 19th-century farmhouse, hidden away in a garden behind high walls in the middle of the village, next to a church. The two rooms are warm and unfussy, with antique country furniture set against pale greens and yellows. Meals are served in a small guests' dining room but are worth staying in for. Raffaella describes her style as "regional home cooking" and she emphasises vegetarian dishes — unusual in Italy. Ingredients are strictly organic and are mostly grown by the family — as is the wine. This area really isn't touristy but you will find plenty to do. It's a great spot for walking and mountain biking — if you aren't scared of hills — and you can horse-ride only one kilometre away. It would be a shame to make this house a mere pit stop — it's worthy of more of your time.

Rooms: 2 D with private bath and shower.
Price: D L80,000; Tr L135,000. Half-board L70,000 p.p. Full-board 90,000 p.p.
Breakfast: Included.
Meals: Lunch/Dinner L38,000 on request.
Closed: Christmas, New Year and 20 June-5 July.

How to get there: From the A21 Torino-Piacenza motorway exit at Villanova d'Asti, follow signs for Buttigliera d'Asti. Continue to Colle Don Bosco Santuario, and follow signs for Montafia. After 1km you arrive in Serra di Capriglio, the house is in the middle of the village beside a little white church.

Map Ref No: 2

Cascina Papa Mora

Via Ferrere 16
14014 Cellarengo AT

Tel: 0141 935 126
Fax: 0141 935 444
E-mail: papamora@tin.it
web: www.itaka.net

Sig.re Adriana & Maria Teresa Bucco

Come for a taste of what it is really like to live on a small farm in Italy — in northern Italy, we should say. Maria Teresa is an enterprising young single parent who runs Cascina Papa Mora with her married sister. She speaks fluent English and will make you feel very welcome. It is as quiet as you could find; the farm concentrates on wine, vegetables and fruit so the only animals you will hear are the frogs in the pond. This is one of Italy's top wine regions, producing the rare Bracchetto (often served to foreign guests by Italian presidents), Barbera, Dolcetto and Spumante, the cheap and cheerful answer to champagne. We can't say that the farmhouse has been lovingly restored — more razed to the ground and rebuilt. However, the bedrooms are pretty, in pink and green chintz, and the bathrooms immaculate, while a pleasant veranda and garden are arranged round the old farm pond. Maria Teresa and her sister also run a restaurant at the farm; they are very serious about their organic credentials and use only seasonal produce. You can have breakfast outside, enjoying the view of the hills, and even the bread is home-made.

Rooms: 5 D/Tw, all en suite.
Price: L50,000 p.p.
Breakfast: Included.
Meals: Lunch on request L20,000; Dinner L20,000. Wine not included.
Closed: 2 January-14 February.

How to get there: On the A21 Torino-Piacenza motorway exit at Villanova d'Asti, follow the signs for Cellarengo. When you arrive on the outskirts of the village turn left into Via Ferrere, continue past small chapel until you reach the farm. The last 300 metres is a well-made stone track.

Map Ref No: 6

Hotel Real Castello

Via Umberto 1, n 9   **Tel:** 0172 470 125
12060 Verduno CN   **Fax:** 0172 470 298

Sig.ra Elisa Burlotto

Yes, it is a real castle, dating from the early 1500s, with sweeping views over the rooftops of the town to the vineyards below. The family of the present owners bought it in 1910 and changed it into an hotel in 1953. Before that, it had an interesting history: for a large chunk of the 19th century it belonged to the royal family and became a popular haunt for some of the young princes. Antiques are everywhere, and many fascinating period details survive, such as original polychrome tiled floors, and a gilt mirror on which young members of the royal household scratched their names with diamond rings — as princelings do. There are also some striking *trompe l'oeil* effects. Senior suites are sumptuous. The cooking is formidable and, if accompanied by the august estate wines famed throughout Piedmont, would certainly whack up the otherwise fairly modest room tariff. The present incumbents are three Burlotto sisters and a lively daughter who run the place with a mix of quiet dignity and panache. In places, the castle is admittedly a bit dilapidated, but it wears its patina of age with dignity.

Rooms: 13: 8 D, 3 Junior Ste, 2 Senior Ste (for 4 people), all en suite.
Price: D L180,000-200,000; Junior Ste L240,000; Senior Ste L300,000.
Breakfast: Included.
Meals: Lunch/Dinner à la carte on request.
Closed: 1 December-14 March.

How to get there: Exit A6 at the Marene Cherasco. Right following signs to Alba. At roundabout in Pollenzo follow signs for Verduno for 6km.

La Saracca

Via Cavour 1
12065
Monforte d'Alba CN

Tel: 0173 787 267
Fax: 0173 787 267

Sig.ri Rosemarie Bernhardt & Giulio Viglione

This 16th-century townhouse in the *centro storico* of Monforte d'Alba seems a promising find. Rosemarie Bernhardt is German, but has lived in Italy for many years and now feels thoroughly at home here. With her partner Giulio, who owns a vineyard near the town, she recently began the conversion of La Saracca into self-catering guest space. This has been a labour of love with painstaking attention to detail. It's a patrician little place of huge charm, and although this is a new venture, we feel confident enough to recommend it on the basis of an enthusiastic inspection report. From the street, which is the oldest in the town, the entrance leads into a pretty courtyard terrace overlooking a narrow valley which makes an attractive, bright, summer dining area. The interior is decorated in pale colours with frescoed ceilings and rococo flourishes. Bedrooms (two on each floor) have separate bathrooms but are intimately arranged, making them perhaps more suitable for families or friends travelling together than for total strangers. Rosemarie and Giulio live just across the road, so are on hand if you need help.

Rooms: 2 + 1 Apt: 2 D, both en suite.
1 Apt for 2-4.
Price: L100,000.
Breakfast: Self-catering.
Meals: Self-catering.
Closed: December and January.

How to get there: From Alba follow signs to Baroco, then to Monforta d'Alba. In the main piazza turn left following signs to Hotel Villa Beccaris. After 0.5km this road continues up; take the lower left fork and swing round back and down to Via Cavour 1.

Lombardy

"Beauty is an experience, nothing else. It is not a fixed
pattern or an arrangement of features. It is something *felt*."
D H Lawrence

Villa Simplicitas & Solferino
22028 San Fedele d'Intelvi CO   **Tel:** 031 831 132/ 02 498 9158

Sig. M. Castelli

A rough tarmac track leads up the mountainside from San Fidele to this romantic retreat in a handsome 18th-century villa surrounded by pastureland and chestnut woods, farmed by the estate's tenants. The tinkling of cowbells is one of the few sounds you're likely to hear; local herds provide the hotel with its dairy produce, and at some later stage in their career, its salami. One of the best features of the house is the view, a spectacular one of Lake Como 800 metres below the sunny terrace. Inside, the villa is elegantly furnished with antiques and a splendid old snooker table. Dashing *trompe l'oeil* decorations festoon some of the walls. There's ample sitting space. Bedrooms are immaculately kept, two with access to a large first-floor terrace. Ulla Hagen's 'sophisticated regional' cooking attracts much attention from locals who drop by for dinner. Even dog phobics should enjoy the two alarmingly large Newfoundlands on duty by the entrance, for these are docile and well-mannered to the point of somnolence, adding to the scene of rural bliss. It's the sort of place that makes you, inexplicably, feel at home.

Rooms: 9 D, all en suite.
Price: L90,000 p.p. Children under 6 half price.
Breakfast: Included.
Meals: Lunch L25,000.
Dinner L35,000.
Closed: 10 Oct-May.

How to get there: From Como head north towards Argegno. Turn left passing through San Fedele then after the 1st bus station turn left; follow winding road for 2km up to the villa.

Map Ref No: 2

Grand Hotel Victoria

Lungolago Castelli 7
22017 Menaggio CO

Tel: 0344 320 03
Fax: 0344 329 92
E-mail: hotelvictoria@palacehotel.it
web: www.palacehotel.it

Sig. Paolo Palano

A large, grand resort hotel with an impressive lakeside setting — not the sort of place usually mentioned in these pages, but with distinct advantages. It dates from the late 19th century and both its architecture and interior décor are straight out of the fashionable *belle-époque* and early 20th-century Liberty style. Imposing staircases, ornate light fittings and florid gilding characterise the yawning public salons on the ground floor. Bedrooms (some smaller than you might expect in an hotel of this category) are predictably comfortable and well equipped with hairdryers and all the usual mod cons. Most have good views overlooking Lake Como or the gardens and mountains to the rear. The hotel is professionally managed with efficient, agreeable staff, though it lacks the personal feel of a small, family-run place and is used quite a lot for business and the conference trade. The restaurant dishes up reliable international fare which can be eaten on a waterfront terrace, with piano music on summer evenings. Private parking, an open-air swimming pool, and 'courtesy' bus services may be other reasons for choosing this hotel.

Rooms: 55: 11 S, 38 D, 6 Ste, all en suite.
Price: S L185,000-210,000; D L320,000-360,000; Ste L440,000-600,000.
Breakfast: Included.
Meals: Lunch L50,000. Half board available on request.
Closed: Never.

How to get there: Exit A9 at Como Nord and follow signs for Menaggio on SS340. Pass through the lights in Menaggio keeping to the right. The road meets the main square and then continues along the river. The hotel is 150m from the square.

Map Ref No: 2

Via Ghislanzoni 24

Loc. Vescogna
23885 Calco LC

Tel: 039 508 724
Fax: 02 864 53 229
E-mail: marcadacqua@micronet.it

Sig.ra Marcella Pisacane

A far cry from the fast pace and chic streets of Milan, yet you are just 30 minutes away. If you enjoy the bohemian life you will love it here. Marcella and Franco, lively and intelligent, are artists – she in animation and he a painter; he also has an antiquarian bookshop in Milan. Their home started out in 1600 as the stables of the noble Calchi family and today you enter through a stone archway into a secluded courtyard. It is full of life and character; Franco's bold paintings adorn the walls and every corner is crammed with things that Marcella has picked up at flea markets. Upstairs are two bedrooms, a double with a big old iron bed and then the more contemporary children's room. You may prefer to be private in the next door hay barn converted, using reclaimed materials, into what Marcella calls 'a suite' — big and open plan. The large bedroom has huge windows looking out through the trees to the village below and a glorious bathroom with hand-painted tiles. You may well intend to make day trips to Milan, Bergamo or Lake Como but then again you may not want to step foot out of the village.

Rooms: 3: 1 Tw and 1 Ste, both en suite. 1 D sharing bathroom.
Price: S L85,000; D L75,000; Ste L130,000.
Breakfast: Included.
Meals: Dinner on request.
Closed: Never.

How to get there: Exit A4 at Agrate and follow signs for Vimercate & Lecco. At Calco turn right just after petrol station and follow the road left then right into Via Ghislanzoni. At the top of the hill take the driveway on right of the right hand turn. Through arch into small courtyard. House is on left.

Casa Clelia

Via Corna 1/3
24039 Sotto il Monte Giovanni XXIII BG

Tel: 035 799 133
Fax: 035 791 788

Sig.ra Rosanna Minonzio

We can do no better than quote from the engaging brochure: "The first thing you'll see when you come to us is the main house, set in the middle of the woods. Beyond the main house you'll find the old convent in the rural area with the outhouses, the orchards and the barns. The history of this charming place comes out untouched at first sight. You need only to give a look at the cellars, to their vastity (they cover entirely the surface of the 17th-century villa) and to their magnificence, to see yourself projected in the magic atmosphere of the past." The hotel has been sculpted out of the 11th-century convent, a labour of devotion for Rosanna and Ferruccio; they have sought out old pieces of furniture and objets d'art and have poured their passion for food into the kitchen. One particular treat is the 'taster' menu, whereby you can nibble, guilt free, at numbers of different dishes. There are three resident children, so your own will be welcome, free to run wild in the gardens, orchards and 80,000 square metres of woods. "Delicious dishes and genuine products... for breakfast... to begin the day, in order to move to the surroundings afterwards..."

Rooms: 10: 8 D, 2 Tr all ensuite.
Price: L60,000 p.p.
Breakfast: Included.
Meals: Lunch/Dinner L25,000-L45,000.
Closed: January.

How to get there: Exit A4 at Capriate.
Follow signs to Sotto il Monte. In Sotto il
Monte follow yellow signs to 'Agriturismo
Casa Clelia'.

Cappuccini

Via Cappuccini 54   **Tel:** 030 715 72 54
25033 Cologne Franciacorta BS   **Fax:** 030 715 72 57

Sig.ri Massimo & Rosalba Pelizzari

It must have been a formidable task to restore this old monastery, perched amid olive groves on the slopes of Mount Orfano, but Massimo and Rosalba have done so with such sympathy and ingenuity that many would willingly be cloistered here forever. Happily much remains unchanged; the columned cloister is simply graced with lemon trees and in the corner a small door leads to a spiral stone staircase and up to a narrow corridor with six small doors. The rooms beyond these doors however are beyond the dreams of any monk, with crisp white linen on king-size beds, antique prints and furnishings. The bathroom basins are old marble on antique stands and Massimo understands the luxury of a bath tub. Camouflaged in each room are a fridge, television, phone and a CD player, with some music to play. Downstairs is a labyrinth of rooms including a small lounge with an open fireplace and a huge, illuminated, stained glass panel. The dining room is subtly elegant — the menu is mouth-watering. Instead of breakfast and lunch there is a splendid brunch. The atmosphere of a monastery but one that has been gently coaxed into the 21st century.

Rooms: 6: 5 D, 1 Ste, all en suite.
Price: D L250,000; Ste L300,000.
Breakfast: Brunch L25,000.
Meals: In restaurant à la carte.
Closed: 1-15 January & 5-20 August.

How to get there: Exit A4 at Palazzolo sull'Oglio and follow signs for Cologne. At traffic lights just before Cologne turn left and follow the road out of the village. Cappuccini is on the left. Go through the gates and take the road which winds up to the hotel.

15

Villa Giulia

Viale Rimembranza 20
Largo di Garda
25084 Gargnano BS

Tel: 0365 710 22
Fax: 0365 727 74
E-mail: hvgiulia@gardanet.it
web: www.gardalake.it/hotel-villagiulia

Famiglia Bombardelli

It is Lake Garda you come for, and the views over it from some of the bedrooms. The house itself is as smart as the lake is simply, naturally, beautiful. The level of service — and aspiration — is high (uniformed staff), the seclusion well below the road is intended, and the absence of small children promises peace to those who need it. But if you detect a touch of caution in the above, note that there is no piped music, no jetty for noisy visiting craft, and there is private parking — gold dust in these parts. For those views ask for a lakeside room in the original villa, or forsake the views and go for the ultra-modern mood of the mini-suites across the well-tended garden. The Villa, for some, will feel like a private house, though there is a red carpet on the paved walkway to the front door — protection from high heels? The dining room, highly modernised in expensive taste, is upstaged by the outside eating area with its backdrop of lakes and mountains. Come and be cosseted, dress for dinner — you may meet a few glitterati.

Rooms: 25 D, all en suite.
Price: S L170,000; D L290,000-380,000.
Breakfast: Included.
Meals: Hotel restaurant à la carte.
Closed: October-Easter.

How to get there: On entering Gargnano from Salo, after the 'Agip' petrol station take the lane to the right. The Villa is at the end of street on the right.

Hotel du Lac
Via P. Coletta 21
25084 Villa di Gargnano BS

Tel: 0365 711 07
Fax: 0365 710 55

Sig. Valerio Arosio

We scoured the lakes for a special place and we found Hotel Du Lac right on the edge of Lake Garda. This narrow and endearing turn-of-the-century townhouse is on the same street as Villa Igea where D.H. Lawrence wrote *Twilight in Italy*. The ox-blood red façade with white relief and green shutters is as striking as the glorious view from the tiny patio that overhangs the lake. The Arosio family have striven to keep the hotel like a family home. The rooms are small but neat, with Victorian and Liberty fixtures and furnishings and floral friezes; the only weaknesses are the small cubicle bathrooms. Six of the twelve rooms look out onto the lake and have little balconies from which you can enjoy this subtropical climate even in October. The small dining room, enclosing a central courtyard with a massive palm which seems to disappear into the clouds, looks directly onto the lake. You may also dine upstairs on the open terrace with fancy metal tables and chairs shaded by an arbour of kiwi, somewhat romantic under starlight with the gentle lapping of the water and the twinkling lights across the lake. There's a small music room with an upright piano just in case you feel moved to tinkle.

Rooms: 12 D, all en suite.
Price: L55,000-80,000 p.p.
Breakfast: Included.
Meals: Restaurant à la carte.
Closed: Mid-October — Easter.

How to get there: Take 45 bis to Villa (di Gargnano) and take slip road down to lake. From here turn left into Via P. Colletta. Permanent parking is 100m from the hotel at Hotel Gardenia.

Map Ref No: 3

Villa San Pietro

Via San Pietro 25
25018 Montichiari BS

Tel: 030 961 232
Fax: 030 998 1098
E-mail: ducroz@unipoint.it
web: www.art-with-attitude.com/villa/san_pietro

Sig.ri Jacques & Annamaria Ducroz

A rather grand name for a house that is one of a line of undistinguished 17th-century terraced houses, but once the front door is opened you will know why we have included it in this book. The entrance is stylish and bright, leading to a large family home. Anna — vivacious and energetic — is married to a Frenchman, has a young child and parents who live in self-contained splendour at the far end of the house. She lived in the USA for a time and has a touch of the glamour that can result (she runs a beauty salon). Her US-style energy and Jacques' relaxed mood (he is a keen cycle fan — does that explain it?) make for a pair of immensely hospitable hosts. The guests have their own *salotto* (sitting room) with a frescoed ceiling and good Italian antique furniture. The bedrooms are immaculate, with a mix of new and antique furniture. The most exceptional thing about the house is the large garden and terrace; there is also a pretty ground-floor *loggia* for some memorable *al fresco* meals (Annamaria's dinners are pretty sophisticated 'regional' affairs, we imagine). Montichiari is no great shakes but has a small *centro storico*.

Rooms: 3 D, all en suite.
Price: S L90,000; D L140,000;
Tr L180,000.
Breakfast: Included.
Meals: Dinner L45,000.
Closed: Never.

How to get there: From Milan motorway
A4 exit at Brescia east. Follow signs for the
centre of the city where there is a very
visible cathedral. Via S. Pietro leads off
corner of central piazza.

Map Ref No: 3

Le Sorgive Le Volpi

Via vicinale delle sorgive
Via Piridello 6
46040 Solferino MN

Tel: 0376 854 252
Fax: 0376 855 256
E-mail: sorgive@gvnet.it
web: aziende.gvnet.it/lesorgive

Sig. Vittorio Serenelli

Although one can't deny the beauty of Lake Garda it's a relief to escape from the hotels, traffic and ice cream parlours to the open land of Lombardy. This 19th-century *cascina* with ochre-washed façade and green shutters has been in the Serenelli family for two generations. The exterior, crowned with pierced dovecote and flanked by carriage house and stables with beautiful wide open arches, remains impressive, even if a little of its character has been lost during restoration. Le Sorgive is still a working 28-hectare family farm with vines, cereal crops and livestock; the eight big rooms each bear the name of female descendants of the family and have a mixture of ancestral and and modern furnishings. Farm produce is on sale: home made jams and preserves, salami and wine. Vittorio's sister Anna has another piece of the estate Cascina Le Volpe, just down the road, where you can taste local food: hand rolled *gnocchi*, traditional mantovan sausages and mouth-watering fruit tarts. There are also riding stables, bicycles, a small gym and a pool.

Rooms: 8 D/Tw, all en suite.
Price: L70,000-90,000 p.p.
Breakfast: Included.
Meals: Dinner L25,000-40,000.
Closed: Never.

How to get there: Exit the A4 Milano-Venezia at Desenzano. Follow signs towards Castiglione and then to Mantova. Solferino is signposted to the left off the main road. Le Sorgive Le Volpi is on left before town.

Map Ref No: 3

Trebisonda
Stada Tononi 92   **Tel:** 0376 809 381
Loc. Trebisonda
46040 Monzambano MN

Sig.ra Valeria Moretti

Lie in the grass, read a book, drink a bottle of wine and dream of your next easy trip to the exquisite Lake Garda. It is not far. But you can banish any lingering feeling of guilt at being idle. The house was probably begun in the 15th century and is now the sort of place that might find itself in the *Architect's Journal* or *Country Living* magazine — done in perfect, understated, good taste. It is simple, and young at heart. The peace is only punctuated by distant bells, the rolling countryside by distant mountains. The bedrooms are big, uncluttered, full of space and light. Our inspector described the décor as "a mixture of old and Ikea, Conran and *objets trouvés*". Valeria is a delight, gentle yet sparkling. They are both passionate about horses, and breed them. But it is best not to bring small children, for the mares and foals need to be quiet. Breakfast is taken in the main house, in a big open-plan dining room/kitchen; it is a feast of organic honeys and home-made jams — definitely not a traditional Continental breakfast.

Rooms: 1 + 2 Apt: 1 D with bathroom,
2 Apt for 2.
Price: for 2 L100,000; for 3 L125,000; for 4
L150,000.
Breakfast: Included for rooms.
Meals: Not available.
Closed: January.

How to get there: From Monzambano follow signs to Volta Mantovana to Olfino. At crossroads, shortly after village, turn left towards Roverbella and Valeggio S.M. Follow for approx. 1.2km, left towards Trebisonda, then left again towards Az. Ag. Trebisonda

Map Ref No: 3

Monte Perego
Strada Francesa Est 41
Loc. Rivalta
46040 Rodigo MN

Tel: 0376 653 290
Fax: 0376 654 027
E-mail: peregomn@tin.it

Sig.ra Marisa Galli

One can't help but smile wryly at the name Monte Perego when all around appears as flat as a pancake, but it was pointed out that there is in fact a little hill on the estate; little it is indeed — blink and you will probably miss it. A tree-lined avenue leads up to the large white farmhouse on the banks of the Osoni River. Marissa and her two daughters, Rita and Federica, busy themselves with the farm and an equestrian school, while Giancarlo her husband lends a helping hand in his free time. If you are lucky he might take you out on the little boat along the river to bird-watch; part of this estate is in a nature reserve and during the summer months there are hoards of ladybirds, a sign that the air is pure and clean. They have given over half of their huge farmhouse to guests who are lodged in either rooms or apartments, all of which are sparklingly new and clean, with en suite bathrooms. Most come to Monte Perego to ride but there is also a large swimming pool at the far end of the villa alongside the little breakfast room and shaded terrace.

Rooms: 4 + 4 Apt: 1 S, 2 D, 1 Tr, all en suite. 4 Apt for 2-4.
Price: S L60,000; D L90,000; Tr L120,000; Apt. L180,000.
Breakfast: Self-catering.
Meals: Not available.
Closed: Never.

How to get there: From Mantova take SP10 towards Cremona. After approx. 5km turn right towards Rodigo. Monte Perego is about 1km beyond Grazie on the right.

Map Ref No: 8

Corte San Girolamo

Strada San Girolamo 1
46100 Mantova MN

Tel: 0376 301 018
Fax: 0376 391 018
E-mail: amantova@mbox.mynet.it

Sig. Kim Soonkee Mantovani

How nice it is to be able to borrow bikes from your host, and potter into the countryside — or even into the town. This is a rather extraordinary place in other ways, a haven just outside Mantova and just inside the Parco del Mincio, with paths leading through it and up to Lake Garda. Do visit the centre of Mantova; it is lovely, with the usual mass of good *osteria*, art and culture (the outskirts are grim). The house is an old water mill, 16th-century, on the site of an old convent, and there is a good feel to the place. Uncle and nephew run it; the former is a painter, writer and poet and somehow the mood comes from him. However, there isn't much contact with the family really; they are all busy on the farm and will leave you to your own devices. The bedrooms (more attractive then the apartments) are comfortable and simple, with old family furniture, and heated in winter (in summer, with so much water about, there are likely to be mosquitoes so bring protection). This is a house for those looking for good value and authenticity, off the beaten track yet close to it.

Rooms: 4 + 2 Apt: 4 D, 2 en suite, 2 sharing bathroom. 2 Apt for 4-5.
Price: S L50,000-L70,000; D L110,000-L130,000. Apt L200,000.
Breakfast: L10,000, on request.
Meals: Dinner L40,000. Saturday only.
Closed: Never.

How to get there: From the Brenero motorway towards Mantova. Exit at Mantova nord towards Mantova cittadela and take the SS236 towards Brescia. After railway crossing turn left towards Soave and then right at the first dirt road on your right.

Corte Schiarino-Lena

Strada Maddalena 7/9
46047 Sant'Antonio di Porto
Mantovano MN

Tel: 0376 398 238
Fax: 0376 393 238
E-mail: villa.schiarino@mbox.mynet.it

Sig. Giuseppe Lena

Part of the fun of creating these books is being able to introduce you to the sort of places that might otherwise go unheeded. This wonderful old lady of a building is 16th-century, built for the Marquis Luigi Gonzaga and little changed but for the inevitable wrinkles. There remains a great threshing floor outside, plus deep arcades and sparsely furnished rooms, just as they once were. Behind the grand façade, with frescoes and wrought iron, there is a touch of emptiness now, though it all comes to life for weddings and receptions. You don't get to live the full grandeur of the place, however, being confined to the cellars (magnificent, with low arched ceiling and huge fireplace, long tables and wooden benches) for your breakfast and some converted outbuildings for your apartments. These are simple and a touch dated, as you'd expect, with a curious mixture of contemporary and period furniture, but the fun is in simply being here, and in roaming the grounds. You may even take a noble stroll through the villa with the owners, and fantasize about a little bolt-hole in Italy.

Rooms: 3 Ste, both en suite.
Price: Ste L170,000-200,000.
Breakfast: Included.
Meals: Not available.
Closed: November — mid-March.

How to get there: Exit A22 at Mantova Nord, follow signs for Mantova until first crossroads, 1.5km after station. Turn right for Verona. Follow canal and turn right for 'Autocisa' way to Verona. After S. Antonio look for sign to 'Palazzetto dello Sport'. Follow Via Gramsci to Via Maddalena.

23

Corte Donda

Loc. Salina di Viadana
46010 Viadana MN

Tel: 0375 785 697
Fax: 0375 85 70 06

Sig. Claudio Rizzi

On the outskirts of a small country village in the flat plains of Emilia Romagna the pink façade of Corte Donda catches the eye. Although recently restored it is very much a working family farm. The wide, long entrance hall is as welcoming as Claudio and his father-in-law, Dante. Both work on the four-hectare smallholding breeding horses, geese and ducks and tending a small vineyard and vegetable garden. Anna, Claudio's wife, and her sister Adriana, work a wonderful kitchen and make pasta and fresh sauces daily. Time your stay for the end of the week when you can eat in the little restaurant; the buffet antipasti is sumptuous. The family lives on the first floor of the house and four big guests rooms are on the top under the eaves of the roof. Although it is all new and shiny they try valiantly to keep a country feel with stippled walls, country-style furniture, floral wall prints and hand-crocheted curtains. Claudio is a passionate collector of old curiosities — you'll see them both inside and outside the house. Do visit the wine cellar — it is an Aladdin's cave — massive wooden doors open to reveal a fascinating array of old wine-making tools.

Rooms: 4D/Tr, all en suite.
Price: S L85,000; D110,000;
Tr L130,000.
Breakfast: Included.
Meals: Dinner L50,000. Wednesday-
Saturday; Lunch on Sunday.
Closed: Never.

How to get there: From Viadana, take main road towards Guastalla. Turn left to Salina. In the village go to right of War Memorial in front of church and immediately left into Via Palazzo. La Corte Donda is well signed on the left. Ring for entry.

Map Ref No: 8

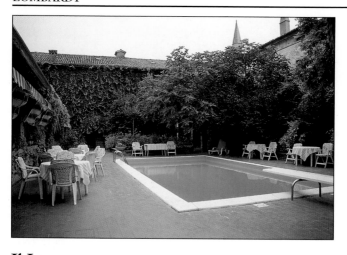

Il Leone

Piazza IV Martiri 2
46030 Pomponesco MN

Tel: 0375 86 145
Fax: 0375 86 770

Sig. Antonio Mori & family

Pomponesco is a sleepy little town in the industrial flatlands of the Padana. The pale pink façade of this simple townhouse reveals nothing. The quiet street leads up to the tall columns of what were once the gates of a park, created as part of an elaborate architectural project. In the rather Bohemian entrance hall your eye darts here and there — dark painted walls, glass chandeliers and paintings — but your attention is drawn to the atrium. Centred on a huge palm, covered in azaleas and rhododendrons, it is a sanctuary for small birds. The main dining room has a painted frieze depicting the four known continents; another has blood-red painted walls and leads to a little nook with an open fireplace. The rooms above the noted restaurant don't quite live up to the standard of the lower floor. The three doubles on the top floor are the nicest; larger and furnished with antiques. Those on the first floor are comfortable and cosy but smaller and more contemporary with floral wall paper and white painted furniture. One of the biggest surprises of all is the swimming pool in an internal courtyard.

Rooms: 5: 1 S, 4 D, all en suite.
Price: S L110,000; D L160,000.
Breakfast: Included.
Meals: Dinner menu à la carte in restaurant.
Closed: January.

How to get there: From A22 exit at Reggiolo Rolo. Follow signs towards Reggiolo and continue to Pomponesco. Il Leone is on the left of the quiet side street that runs from the main square on the far side.

Map Ref No: 8

Trentino Alto
Veneto
Emilia Romagna

"The secret of happiness is curiousity."
Norman Douglas

Hotel Zirmerhof

Redagno di Sopra
39040 Redagno BZ

Tel: 0471 887 215
Fax: 0471 887 225
E-mail: info@zirmerhof.com
web: www.zirmerhof.com

Sig. Josef Perwanger

The sound of music in the peaks of South Tyrol — Alto Adige is a strange area, still more Germanic than Italian, but after all it is a recently acquired possession. The Perwanger family were here when it was still part of Austria and survived all the changes. Sepp, fourth generation, young and enthusiastic, proudly carries on the family tradition. Although Zirmerhof has 32 rooms, once in the small entrance hall you immediately feel at home. There are creaky wooden floors, panelled walls and painted doors — each with a chalked blessing by the priest. The fire burns in the little stone fireplace and family portraits grace the walls — all as *gemütlich* as you can imagine. There is a small library and the Stuber, panelled with a beautiful ceramic wood burning stove, is a snug retreat. Much of the furniture is original to the house including some hundred hand-carved Tyrollean dining chairs! Most of the rooms are big, apart from two minuscule singles, though the rooms in the main building are perhaps a little nicer; they have all recently had new bathrooms of cararra marble. Walking is fabulous here and the views incredible.

Rooms: 32: 4 S, 22 D/Tw, 6 Ste, all en suite.
Price: Half-board: S L117,000-134,000 p.p.; D/Tw L 100,000-148,000 p.p.; Ste L149,000-174,000 p.p.
Breakfast: Included.
Meals: Dinner included. À la carte lunch menu available.
Closed: 8 November -16 December.

How to get there: Exit A22 at Ora and follow signs for Neumarkt, Egna. From here take the steep winding road towards Cavalese & Cortina. After approx 20km turn left for Redagno and follow the road up for a further 9km to Zirmerhof which is to the left just below the village school and church.

Map Ref No: 4

Casa Belmonte

Via Belmonte 2
36030 Sarcedo VI

Tel: 0445 884 833
Fax: 0445 588 4131
E-mail: info@casabelmonte.com
web: www.casabelmonte.com

Sig.ra Mariarosa Arcaro

Elegance and simplicity, perfect taste and seduction — a uniquely Italian gift. The house, a subtle blend of contemporary and old, is on the top of Belmonte hill overlooking the small town of Sarcedo and in seven hectares of vines and olive groves. Mariarosa, dark and petite, has turned her full attention and talents to creating five luxurious rooms now that her children have flown the nest. Monogrammed sheets and towels, even slippers, and bathrobes for each guest are in each sumptuously decorated room along with rich drapes and antique furniture and prints. The bathrooms are decorated with small mosaic tiles with marble surrounds. Delicious breakfasts — yogurts, fruit, cheeses and hams — are served in the little glass garden room. Guests have free range of the grounds and there is also a large pool. Roberto is very proud of the small wine cellar. He has selected the best wines from all over Italy which he reserves for his most important of guests. Casa Belmonte is an easy launch pad for forays to Venice, Padova, Verona and Piacenza.

Rooms: 5: 1 S, 2 D, 1 Tw, 1 Ste,
all en suite.
Price: S L200,000-250,000; Tw/D
L250,000-300,000;
Ste L350,000-450,000.
Breakfast: L25,000-40,000.
Meals: Available on request.
Closed: Never.

How to get there: From A31 exit at
Dueville. Take a left and left again for
Bassano. Continue for approx 2km and turn left for Sarcedo. The entrance to the house is 600m after the traffic lights to the right of the junction. Ring the bell at the gate to enter.

Map Ref No: 4

Il Castello

Via Castello 6
36021 Barbarano VI

Tel: 0444 886 055
E-mail: ilcastello@tin.it

Sig.ra Elda Marobin Marinoni

A narrow, winding road leads up to the foothills of the Berici hills where Il Castello proudly stands. Also known as Villa Godi-Marinoni, the castle was built by Count Godi in the 15th century on the ruins of an old feudal castle. The arched entrance way with its cobbled paving introduces you to the comforting and pervasive sense of great age that wraps itself around Il Castello. The main villa is still lived in by the Marinoni family; Signora Marobin Marinoni and her son run this vast estate together. An annexe with curious gothic details in the plastered façade now houses guests in three apartments and a suite. The furniture is a mix of old and new, antique and contemporary with, for example, a wonderful old *lit bateau* in one suite. Hidden below the castle walls is an Italian garden centred on a fish pond; during the spring and summer months, hundreds of lemon trees are wheeled out to stand grandly on pedestals. The climate is mild and the hill side is a mass of olive groves. Wine is also produced on the estate and there is a vast wine cellar in the bowels of the castle. Take a bottle and retreat to the peace and tranquility of the lemon garden.

Rooms: 4 Apt for 2-4.
Price: L245,000-280,000 p.p. per week.
Breakfast: Self-catering.
Meals: Self-catering.
Closed: Never.

How to get there: Exit A4 at Vicenza Est and take SS247 to Noventa. At traffic lights in Ponte Barbarabi turn right into a narrow road for Barbarano (also indicated Villa Godi). After the sharp right hand bend in centre of village turn left and follow the road up to the villa, approx. 500m on the left.

Map Ref No: 4

Antica Torre

Case Bussandri 197
Loc. Cangelasio
43039 Salsomaggiore Terme PR

Tel: 0524 575 425
Fax: 0524 575 425

Sig. Francesco Pavesi

Vanda and Francesco, he an ex-civil engineer, speak better French or Spanish than English, but don't let that put you off; they are kind, congenial — rather than flamboyant — hosts. The Torre Antica is deeply ancient, built in 1350. Even earlier, there was a salt store here, built for local monks. The tower has three rooms, each with a bathroom and small sitting area with wooden benches made comfortable by cushions. There is a fridge too, and a billiards room with open fireplace. The stairs in the tower are spiral — not great for children or for lugging huge cases. Francesco and Vanda don't encourage guests to bring their children; this might be more of a place for those wanting a quiet time in the country. The other rooms are in the house, with well-polished old furniture against white walls. Vanda does most of the cooking and will make up a picnic for lunch. Meals are eaten in a converted barn. Breakfast is Continental with a few extras. Another barn has been turned into a dayroom for guests but is a touch bleak, as is the flat. The pool is a great distraction, as are the mountain bikes. A quiet, gentle place.

Rooms: 9: 1 S, 8 D/TW, all en suite.
Price: B&B: L65,000 p.p. Half-board:
L90,000 p.p.
Breakfast: Included.
Meals: Available.
Closed: 30 November-1 March.

How to get there: From centre of
Salsomaggiore take SP27 for Cangelasio
and Piacenza. On leaving Salsomaggiore
fork left (signed Cangelasio). After approx.
1.6km turn left signposted Antica Torre. Drive is on left after another 1.5km.

Az. Ag. Beneverchio
Via Niviano 31   **Tel:** 0536 325 290
41026 Pavullo nel Frignano MO

Sig.ra Claudia Ori

It's well worth taking a detour to stay at Beneverchio and not only for the breathtaking views across the wooded hills to the valley below and up again to the Abetone mountains. It was originally built as lodging for priests and pilgrims; now your hosts, genuine and humble country folk, pour heart and soul into making this a friendly little hostelry. Claudia is the driving force, helped by her mother and her partner Ornello who, aside from looking after the farm, is also on call for whatever else needs doing. There are six rooms in the main house and another three in the annexe, simple but with good firm mattresses to ensure a restful night. There is also a sitting room with various relics, such as a framed group of old keys and an old sewing table and machine, but Claudia's great pride is her kitchen and little dining room. The food is diverse and delicious and fit for Gargantua: home-made breads, antipasti, a trio of pastas, two main courses — and you must leave room for the home-made desserts, all washed down with local wine and a *digestivo*. Just as well the rooms are close at hand.

Rooms: 9 D, all en suite.
Price: L135,000 p.p.
Breakfast: Included.
Meals: Dinner L35,000.
Closed: Never.

How to get there: From Pavullo take SS12 south towards Abetone. Towards the end of the town turn left for Niviano & Montorso. Zigzag up the hill passing a house with a mural decoration following signs for Niviano. Beneverchio is on the right approximately 3km from Pavullo.

           Map Ref No: 8

Az. Ag. La Fenice
Via S. Lucia 29
Ca' de Gatti
40040 Rocca di Roffeno BO

Tel: 051 919 272
Fax: 051 919 27

Sig. Remo Giarandoni

Remo and Paolo are brothers and were born at La Fenice. Anything but 'country bumpkins', they have taken the farm in an unusual direction: growing seed potatoes for export. Their land is therefore officially 'closed' to other crops. The brothers did much of the renovation themselves and you are likely to find them in overalls working on their latest project, perhaps the pool. La Fenice is a bit of a jigsaw puzzle; you will want to explore it. Most bedrooms have their own outside door and some have an open fireplace and a supply of wood. The rooms are rather like spare rooms in a big house with an assortment of furniture that hangs together well, a masculine touch here and there. They are a bit dark, as the windows are small and some ceilings are low, so prepare to duck. Breakfast is the usual: plenty of coffee, or possibly tea or chocolate, with bread or brioches but Remo and Paolo aren't keen on being confined to breakfast and you, too, would regret it: this region is admired in Italy for having the best cooking in the country. Riders can take out one of the Anglo-Arab horses; a qualified instructor is on hand in the summer.

Rooms: 10 D, all en suite.
Price: B&B: D L120,000-130,000. Half-board: L160,000 — L180,000 p.p.
Breakfast: Included.
Meals: Half-board available.
Closed: January.

How to get there: Take SS64 south from Bologna. After 30km turn right for Tole. From Tole follow signs for Cereglio, after approx. 1.5km turn right. La Fenice is approx. 5km from Tole on the right.

Map Ref No: 8

Az. Ag. Belle Lu

Via Banzi 1   **Tel:** 051 807 034
40050 Fraz. Bagnarola di Budrio BO   **Fax:** 051 807 078

Sig.ra Maria Grazia Gardani

It's true that the pylons are a little startling but Maria Grazia will soon put you at your ease with her warm and genuine welcome. She lives and breathes the little farm; it is her life and soul and you're likely to find her in jeans working in the garden or cooking in the kitchen. The house reflects her vivacious character and individual style with a wild and wonderful collection of intriguing bits and pieces; old photos and cooking utensils, large early maps of Europe and America and a cuckoo clock. Steep uneven terracotta stairs lead up to the first floor where there are three bedrooms, another three have recently been opened in an adjacent building. Those in the main house have turn-of-the-century painted wrought iron bedheads, antique furniture and views over the surrounding flat countryside. You can linger in the shade of the pergola in the garden, your children can explore the farm and feed the gaggle of ducks and geese — this is very much Maria Grazias's home but it's totally informal and you can come and go as you please. Although in the peace and quiet of the country you're close here both to the city of Bologna and to the airport.

Rooms: 6: 4 Tw, 1 Tr, 1 Q, all en suite.
Price: L70,000 p.p.
Breakfast: Included.
Meals: Dinner L30,000.
Closed: Never.

How to get there: From Bologna take SS64 heading north. At Osteriola turn right for Budrio. Continue for approx. 9km to Bagnarola.

Map Ref No: 9

La Cisterna
Non si po
Cosi Non Fanno Tutti
Gargilalotta

E-mail: lacisterna@internatinet.net
web: www.cisterna-monsterosa.it

Sig. Cino Beviacqua

Austere, magnificent, clean-limbed and mercifully free of the baroque flimflam that clutters so much functional architecture in Italy. Built for the local landowner, a man clearly obsessed by the potential of drought to ruin his estate, this is a giant cistern; note the bulbous object at the foot of its monumental 'folly'. If you look carefully, however, you will see that a small window has been let into the side of this great, largely underground, structure. In order to make an entrance you have to lift a vast lid, to which a handle has been thoughtfully attached, then clamber down a ship's ladder to the rounded bottom. It would be to spoil the surprise to say any more. Anyway, it is a common delusion that one can make things better just by writing about them. This structure reminds us of Frank Lloyd Wright's dictum that we should learn from the snail, for it has devised a home both exquisite and functional. And remember, too, that there is no problem so big or intractable that cannot be solved by merely running away from it.

Rooms: 1 multi, fully en suite.
Price: L10, if you can track down Sig. Beviacqua.
Breakfast: D.I.Y., using locally sourced materials.
Meals: Picnics welcome (bring a plastic bag).
Closed: Never.

How to get there: Find the field, then follow your nose.

Ca' Monti

Via Montemorosino 4
Loc. Sassoleone
40025 Fontanelice BO

Tel: 0542 976 66
Fax: 0542 976 66

Sig. Giuliano Monti

The Monti family pride themselves on their hospitality, and quite rightly so as they've been receiving guests at their farm for over two hundred years. Today it is Guiliano and his sister Lea who manage the 21 hectare farm. Spring here is beautiful when all the apricots are in bloom and deer graze in the open pastures. Half of the house is shaded by a mass of chestnut trees and from the other half are glorious views of the Santerno valley, perfect countryside for those who enjoy the great outdoors. Lea is a fabulous cook and at weekends Ca' Monti really comes to life; the small dining room bustles with activity and it's all hands on deck, mother and other siblings all pitching in. Only the freshest ingredients are used and the local woods are scoured during the autumn for the prized porcini mushrooms and chestnuts. Sleeping here is for the select few as there are only four guest rooms, two on the third floor of the house and another two in the recently restored barn, which are simply but well-decorated in country style. Unwind and enjoy good, genuine food and honest hospitality.

Rooms: 4: 2 D, 2 Q, all en suite.
Price: B&B: L60,000 p.p. Half-board: L85,000 p.p.
Breakfast: Included.
Meals: L45,000.
Closed: 6 January-14 February.

How to get there: From SS610 Fontanelice follow signs to Sassoleone along Via Gesso for approx. 8km. Turn left into Via Montemorosino and continue for another 1.5km to the house.

Map Ref No: 9

Torre Pratesi

Via Cavina 11
Cavina
48013 Brisighella RA

Tel: 0546 845 45
Fax: 0546 845 58
E-mail: torrep@tin.it
web: web.tin.it/torrepratesi

Sig.ri Nerio & Letty Raccagni

Sadly for this beautiful, squat and angular 16th-century tower, but luckily for us, the invention of gun powder rendered it defunct. However, it was roofed and turned into a hunting lodge and a farmhouse was added in 1800. Together they are an impressive sight with equally impressive views. The orangey-pink façade of the house is in pretty contrast to the imposing stone tower. Inside, there is another surprise: a gentle mix of antique and contemporary furnishings, bright coloured red leather armchairs and kilim rugs. Each floor of the tower has a large room, named in honour of the wildlife that frequent the area: *Il Falcone*, the falcon, suitably nested under the eaves, and *Cinghiale*, the wild boar, down on the ground floor. The four suites with little sitting areas, some with an open fireplace, are named after the surrounding mountains. Torre Pratesi is still a working farm and the olive oil, wine, preserves, fruit, vegetables and cheese are put to excellent use in the kitchen. There is also excellent walking, with trails mapped out by the Italian Alpine Club that stretch away from the ridge behind the house.

Rooms: 8: 4D; 3 Ste, all en suite.
Price: D L250,000-300,000;
Ste L300,000-350,000.
Half-board: L200,000-225,000 p.p.
Breakfast: Included.
Meals: Dinner L75,000-85,000.
Closed: 10-25 January.

How to get there: From Brisighella
continue through Fognano. Turn right just
after village and take SP63 for 3km to
Torre Pratesi.

Liguria

"...nobody really likes capers no matter what you do with them. Some people *pretend* to like capers, but the truth of the matter is that any dish that tastes good with capers in it, tastes even better with capers not in it."

Nora Ephron

Torri Superiore

Via Torri Superiore 5
18039 Ventimiglia IM

Tel: 0184 215 290
Fax: 0184 215 390
E-mail: torrisup@rosenet.it
web: www. ecovillages.org

Sig. Massimo Candela

Eco-tourism with a difference, run by a non-profit-making venture to create a sustainable alternative community. Members cook and eat together and share the tasks of restoring and maintaining the gorgeous stone medieval village in which they live. Torri Superiore is a single but complex building, a maze of steps and passages linking over 160 rooms. These are variously used as communal or guest rooms, offices or living space for a cosmopolitan range of about 20 permanent residents shunning city life in favour of rural harmony. Period features have been carefully kept; there are thick walls, vaulted ceilings, and small windows with pale green shutters. Most people who live here are in their 30s and 40s, friendly, interesting and much-travelled folk. They're committed, but uncranky — there's no 'party line' to tow. Younger visitors come here for working holidays; older guests are welcome to join in or simply enjoy the beautiful surroundings. This place is neither for the anti-social nor the hedonistic; don't expect mod cons, room service or private bathrooms, and bring your own towel.

Rooms: 5 D/Tw, sharing bathroom.
Price: B&B: L40,000 p.p. Full-board: L60,000 p.p. Half-board: L50,000 p.p.
Breakfast: Included.
Meals: Lunch/Dinner L10,000; Wine L5,000.
Closed: Never.

How to get there: From Ventimiglia follow signs for Bevera and Torri after 8km. In Torri Inferiore, cross the river and turn into Via Rivaira at the end of the road turn left into Via Torri Superiore, proceed to the end of the road.

Map Ref No: 6

Via Garibaldi 44
18039 Ventimiglia IM

Tel: 0184 238 008
Fax: 0184 238 008

Carolyn McKenzie

The slightly shabby exterior deceives you, as so often in Italy. And as you climb the gloomy stairs to Carolyn's you may wonder if you have made the right choice. But take courage and press on, for there are fresh paint and pictures on the landing on her floor and she does have electricity and running water. Carolyn's part of the house, in the medieval quarter, was added in 1908, with the kitchen, bathroom and terrace squeezed into the 16th-century ramparts. *Alta*, as it is known, is unspoilt by tourism so still has a village atmosphere. From the terrace, where you can see the sea and much of the town, you can enjoy the street life below without being seen. The street is closed to traffic during the week so there is plenty going on. The bedroom is large with white walls. You are only 10km away from the French border and the hills behind the town are full of interesting old villages. If Carolyn is not teaching in it, you are welcome to settle down in the living room — just don't smoke! But there's much to do; how about a swim? The sea awaits at the end of a many-stepped descent.

Rooms: 1 D with shared bathroom.
Price: L35,000 p.p.
Breakfast: Included.
Meals: Use of kitchen available.
Closed: From time to time throughout the year, so do book ahead.

How to get there: Leave A10 at Ventimiglia and follow signs towards Museo-Forte Annunziata. The road winds up around foot of old town and behind.
Just before the museum take a very sharp right back into Piazza Funtanin and park car. Walk under archway into Via Garibaldi; number 44 is first door on the left.

Map Ref No: 6

I Maccario 'Il Bausco'

Loc. Brunetti
18033 Camporosso IM

Tel: 0184 206 013
Fax: 0184 206 851

Sig. Adriano Maccario

A photogenic hillside setting above a small quiet hamlet gives this place much of its charm. Il Bausco is a good base for exploring the attractive Nervia valley and its close-packed clusters of pantiled mountain villages. Il Bausco's buildings aren't especially pretty from a distance, but reveal plenty of homely rusticity at close quarters. Most interesting, perhaps, is the 'little house' up rough stone steps; this has an ancient wood oven which guests may use if they're feeling adventurous and are unlikely to cause a conflagration. The 'big house' is roomy with a bright sun terrace and two large bedrooms. Both houses are furnished with an eclectic mix of traditional farmhouse pieces, which give an air of genuine rural personality. A thoughtful touch — all the windows are fitted with mosquito netting. The family lives down in the town of Dolceacqua attending to their winery, organic farm and shop, but visit regularly to feed the poultry and rabbits and to see that everything's running smoothly. Adriano is a keen environmentalist, knowledgeable about the herbs and medicinal plants that grow in the area. Note that unguarded steps could be a hazard for children or elderly visitors.

Rooms: 3 Apt: 2 for 4, 1 for 2.
Price: L35,000-45,000 p.p.
Breakfast: Self-catering.
Meals: Self-catering.
Closed: February.

How to get there: From Bordighera or Ventimiglia follow signs for Dolceacqua. After Dolceacqua, left towards Rochetta, then left towards La Colla, Gouta, Camporosso. At intersection keep to extreme left and follow signs for Az. Ag.Terre Bianche. Approx. 1km after Terre Bianche right, follow signs for 'Il Bausco' which is on the right on entering the hamlet.

Terre Bianche-Locanda del Bricco

Loc. Arcagna
18035 Dolceaqua IM

Tel: 0184 314 26
Fax: 0184 312 30
E-mail: terrebianche@terrebianche.com
web: www.terrebianche.com

Sig. Paolo Rondelli

Deep in the vine-clad terraces of the Nervia Valley, Terre Bianche was a military barracks, built in the 1930s. Pillaged for building materials after World War II, it owes its recent transformation to the Rondelli family. Paolo is a builder, now heavily involved with the estate's production of DOC Rossese, a red wine named after the local rocky terrain and a great favourite of Napoleon. There's other home-grown produce on the menu too, including olive oil, herbs, and jams from over a hundred varieties of fruit tree. The largest and most interesting bedrooms are in the general's house, though the splendid sea-view dining room directly overhead may make these a bit noisy if the wine is flowing freely over dinner. Ground-floor barracks rooms are smaller, darker and perhaps more spartan, but each has its own entrance and a little grassy patio with garden furniture. Hidden amid the vines is the stone-built Casa della Mimosa, a self-contained annexe popular with honeymooners. Paolo is an engaging and cultivated host who has travelled widely. He's keen on shooting, and will have you blazing away at flying saucers if that's your thing.

Rooms: 10: 3 D, 3 Tr, 4 Q, all en suite.
Price: B&B: L90,000-110,000.
Half-board: L120,000-140,000 p.p.
Full-board: L160,000 p.p.
Breakfast: Included.
Meals: Dinner L30,000; wine from
L18,000.
Closed: November and January after
Epiphany.

How to get there: From Bordighera or
Ventimiglia follow signs for Dolceacqua. Beyond Dolceacqua left for Rochetta and left again at signpost for La Colla, Camporosso and Valley Roja. At intersection take extreme left fork and follow for about 2km. The hotel is on the right.

Map Ref No: 6

Baia La Ruota

Via Madonna della Ruota 34
18012 Bordighera IM

Tel: 0184 266 555/426 5222
Fax: 0184 262 290
E-mail: ruota@ruota.it
web: www.ruota.it

Sig. Gian Quinto Meli

Madonna della Ruota, or Our Lady of the Wheel, refers to a millwheel that accidentally rolled down the hillside, coming to rest on the shore without hurting anyone. A chapel to the Madonna was built on the spot in thanksgiving. In 1855, a local, Giovanni Ruffini, put Baia della Ruota on the map when he wrote *Doctor Antonio* while in exile in England. This romantic, patriotic novel became so popular that English people flocked to Bordighera to see the places he so lovingly described. Gian Quinto, who has been here for 15 years, puts a lot of thought into making the village a special place for families with children. The simply furnished white cabins are dotted among the olive groves and gnarled old trees have been used to support the canopies that shade some patios. The small beach, with umbrellas and deckchairs, is sheltered by a long breakwater — great swimming for children. If you don't want to cook, you can eat at the restaurant or take food back to your cabin. A bus stops outside the gate to take you to Bordighera with its ice creams and shops, or perhaps to the market along the seafront.

Rooms: 32 Apts: 20 for 2, 3 for 3 and 9 for 4.
Price: For 2 L650,000-1,250,000, for 3 L850,000-1,550,000; for 4 L1,100,000-1,950,000 per week. Shorter periods on request.
Breakfast: L12,000.
Meals: Lunch L35,000. Dinner L35,000.
Closed: 1 November-31 March.

How to get there: Very clearly signposted on the seaward side of the main road in Bordighera towards 'ospedaletti'. About half-way between the two (3km from either) follow the steep concrete drive.

Map Ref No: 6

Villa Elisa

Via Romana 70
18012 Bordighera IM

Tel: 0184 261 313
Fax: 0184 261 942
E-mail: villaelisa@masterweb.it
web: www.villaelisa.com

Sig. Maurizio Oggero

Come at any time of the year. Maurizio and Rita take huge pleasure in showing you the natural beauty and artistic heritage of the area. Maurizio takes groups off into the Maritime Alps or along the coast in the hotel minibus and guides them back on three-to-five hour walks. Horse-riding can also be organized. Rita describes looking after her guests and making sure they are happy as her 'hobby' rather than her job. Artists come here to paint, following in the footsteps of Monet. The hotel was built in the '20s when Bordighera, a pretty town, with sloping tree-lined roads and ornate, pastel houses, was a quiet spot to spend the winter months. Maurizio's father, who ran the hotel for many years, was a keen painter and liked having artists to stay; bedroom walls are hung with the pictures they left him. Children are in their element here. When you manage to get them out of the pool, the large airy playroom is full of dolls, toys and games. In midsummer, activities are organized for them too. The pebbled beach is a 10-minute walk down the hill and across the railway, which, strangely, seems to blend in well here.

Rooms: 35 + 1 Apt: 5 S, 30 D, all en suite; 1 Apt for 4 (1 Tw, 1 D).
Price: S L125,000-170,000; D L160,000-250,000.
Breakfast: Included.
Meals: Lunch L50,000; Dinner L50,000-60,000. Half/full board available for weekly stays.
Closed: 5 November-20 December.

How to get there: Via Romana runs parallel to the main road through town (Via Aurelia), reachable by any of the crossroads that link the two. Villa Elisa is at the western end of Via Romana.

41

La Crosa

Fraz. Crosa 10
17030 Vendone SV

Tel: 0182 763 31
Fax: 0182 763 31
E-mail: lacrosa@infocomm.it

Sig. Luigi Bodini

Olives are the main ingredient here; the house is surrounded by olive trees. But you can smell other things too: the grapes ripening on the pergola, Alessandra's cakes, the oven. The one remaining tower of the nearby ruined 14th-century castle overlooks the valley, and the hill is dotted, too, with gigantic stone 'totem' poles created by a local German sculptor; you may find yourself watching him at work. There is a lovely atmosphere, with the delightful Alessandra and Luigi half the attraction; guests return year after year and obviously feel utterly at home. The house is more than 600 years old, the oldest in the hamlet. A mule trail used to pass by but now goes under the house via an arch built by Luigi. There is a lot of wildlife (boar, badgers, fox and hares come into the garden), many walking trails, and the town of Alberga has some interesting things to see, such as a medieval baptistry and two fine museums. There is easy access to beaches and Genoa is only an hour away by train. A wonderful place to combine sea, culture and walking... and there are mountain bikes here, too.

Rooms: 4 Apt: for 2-6.
Price: L100,000-120,000. Half-board: L75,000-85,000 p.p.
Breakfast: Included.
Meals: Lunch L5,000 (light buffet); Dinner L25,000.
Closed: During winter.

How to get there: Exit A10 at Albenga and follow signs for Pieve di Teco. After approx. 5km turn right at signpost for 'La Crosa' at intersection.

Map Ref No: 6

Villa Piuma

Via Cappeletta Nuova 8
Loc. Perti
17024 Finale Ligure SV

Tel: 0196 870 30
Fax: 0196 870 30

Sig.ra Marida Provenzani

This magnificent 18th-century villa in *rosso inglese* was built on to a 15th-century watch-tower. Inhabited until the 1960s by titled aristocrats, the villa fell into disrepair until the enterprising and energetic Marida acquired it in 1992. She has lovingly and meticulously restored it and this is D.I.Y. elevated to an art form: chastely decorated rooms in imaginative colour combinations show off the restored antiques beautifully, and a charming effect is created by touches such as hand-stencilled friezes of elephants or ducks, and by the presence of two dogs and five cats. Marida also runs the farm single-handed, producing olives, vegetables and wine (free with her excellent meals!) and caring for her livestock. Yet she loves spending time with her guests and making them feel at home. Eating arrangements and pricing structures are as flexible as Marida herself. Two rooms look out over the garden and the valley beyond, while the third, up steep stairs, surveys craggy rocks: the motorway below them emits a faint hum. There's plenty to do close at hand, from fishing and mountain climbing to ping-pong in the garden.

Rooms: 3 D, all en suite.
Price: L35,000-40,000 p.p. (minimum stay 6 days during summer).
Breakfast: Light continental L2,500.
Meals: Dinner, 3 times a week during the summer, L25,000-30,000.
Closed: 3 January-28 February.

How to get there: Exit A10 at Finale Ligure. At the first intersection left and left again. From Finale Borgo continue for 3km towards Palestra di Roccia and Calice Ligure. Right at the 'Az. Ag. Villa Piuma' signpost in Via Cappeletta Nuova, it is the second house on right.

Map Ref No: 7

Cascina del Vai

Strada Ville 4
17014 Cairo Montenotte SV

Tel: 019 508 94
Fax: 019 508 94

Sig. Alberto Becattini

A ranch-style gateway makes an imposing entrance to this peaceful rural property amid fields and woods. Hard-working Alberto has converted the farm buildings, once very run-down, into practical, modern units with spanking new, en suite, bathrooms. All of these have natural light and are quiet and clean, though the bedrooms, it must be said, are a bit short on character. The exterior of the building, however, has many handsome period features. There's plenty of public space inside and out, including a huge, dark-timbered dining room, a large bar and a massive barbecue area. Hearty regional cooking is a plus point, and the restaurant, which seats up to 80, pulls in a lot of keen eaters, especially at weekends. Alberto's managerial style is very much hands-on; besides running the place virtually single-handed, he's also the chef and the menu revolves around his own ranch-raised beef. He is also unusually knowledgeable about beers, wines and spirits. One of his other passions is — more noisily — motor-cross rallying. He hopes to convert other buildings into additional bedrooms soon.

Rooms: 5 D/Tw, all en suite.
Price: L50,000 p.p.
Breakfast: Included.
Meals: Lunch L25,000-30,000;
Dinner L25,000-30,000.
Closed: January.

How to get there: From Cairo
Montenotte follow signs for Cortemelia.
After approx. 4km right to 'Localita Ville',
follow these signs to the end of the road.

Map Ref No: 7

Palazzo Fieschi
Piazza della Chiesa 14
16010 Savignone GE

Tel: 010 936 0063
Fax: 010 936 821
E-mail: fieschi@split.it
web: www.fieschi.busalla.it

Sig.ri Simonetta & Aldo Caprile

The name of this elegant townhouse near Genoa commemorates former owners, the distinguished Fieschi family, once a significant power in the land. Since 1992, the palazzo has belonged to Simonetta and Aldo Caprile, who swapped careers in the business world of Genoa for a life of hotel-keeping. Settling into their new role with enthusiasm, they have carefully renovated the building, incorporating mod cons into its *cinquecento* grandeur. For all its period interest and long history as an hotel, it feels warm and inviting; very much a family home as well as a thriving business. It stands in the village centre, just across the square from the parish church. The surrounding countryside is green and hilly; it is far from the autostradas and with plenty of good walking nearby. Bedrooms are large and airy, most with heavy curtains and grand beds. Those on the mezzanine floor in the oldest section of the house have most character with tiles, imposing doorways and low ceilings. The Capriles are extremely helpful hosts, and you may encounter the odd musical evening in winter.

Rooms: 20: 4 S, 13 D/Tw, 2 Tr, 1 Q.
Price: S L180,000-190,000;
D/Tw L115,000-125,000 p.p.;
Tr L100,000-105,000 p.p.
Breakfast: Included.
Meals: Lunch/Dinner L50,000-80,000.
Closed: 25 December-25 January.

How to get there: Exit the A7 at Busalla. From Busalla follow signs towards Casella. After 3.5km turn left towards Savignone. The hotel is in the centre of the village.

Map Ref No: 7

Az. Ag. Gnocchi Roberto

Via Romana 53
San Lorenzo della Costa
16038 Santa Margherita Ligure GE

Tel: 0185 283 431
Fax: 0185 283 431

Sig. Roberto Gnocchi

Why bother with Portofino, wondered our inspector, after a visit full of magic to Roberto's villa. It is an idyllic spot, quiet but close to the action. Roberto, a farmer, trained at Pisa University and inherited the house from his grandfather in a very run-down state; it had been let to bad tenants for 20 years. What you now see is the result of 12 years of hard work, including the rebuilding, stone by stone, of many of the terrace walls. They love farming here, deep in the country but within sight of the sea. On a clear day you can see down the coast to the end of the Cinque Terre, perhaps from your horizontal position on a deck-chair in the garden. From here you can do all your sightseeing on foot, a treat indeed. Roberto and Simona are a really lovely couple; both were born, and grew up, in the area. Much of the furniture belonged to the grandparents. There are patchwork quilts on the beds, delicious meals on the table, paths to most of the villages and buses going past the gate to the others. A wonderful spot.

Rooms: 8: 7 D, 1 Q, all en suite.
Price: L75,000 p.p.
Breakfast: Included.
Meals: Dinner L25,000.
Closed: Mid-October — Easter.

How to get there: From Santa Margherita follow signs for S. Lorenzo della Costa for approx 4km. Pass a big sign 'Genova and S. Lorenzo' on left and Autostrada A12 on right, less than 50m ahead take the narrow left. At the red and white barrier ring the bell, as there is another gate further down.

Map Ref No: 7

Hotel Piccolo
Via Duca degli Abruzzi 31
16034 Portofino GE

Tel: 0185 269 015
Fax: 0185 269 621
E-mail: dopiccol@tin.it
web: www.domina.it

Sig. Roberto Tiraboschi

"Only God could have arranged such a spot", was the verdict overheard from one guest. The Hotel Piccolo — not as little as its name suggests — has the only beach around here. Just walk over a little road and you are in a pretty terraced garden leading onto the immaculate pebbled beach in a sheltered cove. The village itself, Italy's answer to St. Tropez, is a five-minute walk away through the pines and olives. Most of the large bedrooms — decorated in an unusual but successful shade of salmon — look out over the sea and many have a terrace or balcony. Once the summer home of a wealthy Genoese family, the Piccolo became a hotel in 1950 and was done up again in 1992. Roberto, the friendly and very helpful manager, will send you off to the market in Santa Margherita or to see the statue of Jesus under the sea off the tiny village of San Fruttuoso. Portofino is tiny and does get awkward for cars in high summer, but it is easy to get around by bus or by boat. If you just want to potter, the hotel offers a set lunch and dinner; the regional cooking is delicious.

Rooms: 22 D/Tw all en suite.
Price: S L180,000-240,000;
D/Tw L240,000-440,000;
Ste L240,000-340,000.
Breakfast: Included.
Meals: Dinner L50,000.
Closed: November to March.

How to get there: Exit A12 at Rapallo.
Follow indications to Santa Margherita
Ligure and Portofino. At Portofino you
will enter Via Provinciale. The hotel is 300m before centre of town.

Map Ref No: 7

Giandriale

Loc. Giandriale 5
19010 Tavarone di Maissana SP

Tel: 0187 840 279
Fax: 0187 840 279
web: www.valdivara.com

Sig.ri Nereo & Lucia Giani

"The fruit trees have been generous to us this year". That remark somehow encapsulates their attitude to their farm and their land; having left Milan they have poured their hearts and souls into the restoration of what was once a very run down property. They have rescued a lot of old farm furniture, much of it in chestnut. The Val di Vara is now a completely protected environmental zone; hunting is forbidden and only organic farming is allowed. To get there you wind your way along a narrow, rough road through the woods. There are terraced pastures for cows, and dense woods all around, so there is a deep sense of isolation and tranquility. Indeed, Lucia and Nereo consider it a place of silence and "nothingness", where guests can join in with farm activities if they wish, or do nothing. Nereo will help you identify flowers and plants, trees and wildlife. Inside, the mood is created by the solidity of the houses, the stone walls, wooden furniture and colourful rugs, the simplicity, the use of cane and bamboo. It is very special place, "number one in absolute", said a local. Come listen to the silence.

Rooms: 6: 3D, 3 Tr, all en suite.
Price: B&B: L40,000 p.p. Half-board:
L65,000 p.p.
Breakfast: Included.
Meals: Dinner L25,000.
Closed: 10 days a year in winter.

How to get there: From Sestri Levante towards Casarza, Castiglione Chiavarese to Missano. Turn left in village just before the church and continue for a further 6km to the house.

Monte Pù

Loc. Monte Pù
16030 Castiglione Chiavarese GE

Tel: 0185 408 027
Fax: 0185 408 027

Sig.ra Aurora Giani

One of our most magical places. It stands, remote and blissfully silent, on the site of a 9th-century Benedictine monastery whose tiny chapel still survives. Surrounded by forest, it's now a 200-hectare farm with cherry and pear orchards and trout ponds (fishing by arrangement). Organic produce is served in its restaurant; rabbits, goats, hens, cows all contribute in their various ways. *Pù* (from Latin *purus*) means pure, referring to the quality of the air and natural spring water and harking back to the purification side of monastic life. Aurora, youthful and vigorous, loves to sit with her guests on summer evenings gazing at the stars, the fireflies and the lights of fishing vessels on the sea far below. One room has an optional kitchen, well equipped but, understandably, seldom used! If you think it worth negotiating the steep, rugged road, Monte Pù is a good base. A minibus to Genoa can be arranged, which can also call at Sestri Levante station. Archery, flower arranging and cookery lessons are offered, and there's a huge sitting/recreation room. The chapel can even be used for weddings, provided the reception is held here too.

Rooms: 10 + 1 Apt: 8 D with private bathrooms, 2 D sharing bathroom. 1 Apt for 2-6.
Price: B&B: L65,000 p.p. Half-board: L90,000 p.p. Apt L220,000.
Breakfast: Included.
Meals: Dinner on request L35,000-L40,000.
Closed: 31 October-Easter.

How to get there: From Sestri Levante towards Casarza. Aprox. 1km beyond Casarza, left to Massasco and Campegli. Monte Pù is just before Campegli.

49

Map Ref No: 7

Hotel Villa Edera

Via Venino 12
16030 Moneglia GE

Tel: 0185 492 91
Fax: 0185 494 70
E-mail: h.edera@pn.itnet.it
web: www.villaedera.com

Sig. Pasquale Schiaffino

Not pretty and not quiet — trains pass rather close. We did wonder. The Villa Edera is perched above the village of Moneglia and reached through five low, narrow tunnels: an adventure for some, daunting for others. Regulars often come by train and walk, but staff would be happy to pick you up. Once you find the hotel and settle in you will start to appreciate it; Villa Edera is a true family hotel. The Schiaffinos have been in Moneglia for almost 300 years and are passionate about "their" village. Orietta, the elder daughter, manages the hotel yet still finds time to sing in a choir. She especially enjoys meeting people who share her love of music. Her husband and her sister's husband are waiters; her mother Ida is a brilliant cook, preparing Ligurian dishes with fresh organic produce. Her father, Lino — who should be resting as he has had heart trouble — will fuss over you making sure everything is going smoothly. Orietta is also a keen walker and enjoys taking guests out for some serious walking. But you may prefer to catch a boat to Portofino or the Cinque Terre.

Rooms: 27: 2 S, 23 Tr, 2 Q, all en suite.
Price: B&B: S L100,000-140,000 p.p.;
D L65,000-90,000 p.p. Half board:
L88,000-130,000 p.p.
Breakfast: Included.
Meals: Lunch/Dinner L30,000-40,000.
Closed: 5 November-1 March.

How to get there: Exit A12 at Sestri Levante, follow signs for Moneglia Tunnel. Immediately after 5th tunnel turn right (at sports field) and follow signs for Hotel Villa Edera.

Agriturismo Villanova

Loc. Villanova
19015 Levanto SP

Tel: 0187 802 517
Fax: 0187 802 517
E-mail: massola@iol.it
web: www.agrivillanova.com

Barone Giancarlo Massola

Villanova is where Barone Giancarlo Massola's ancestors spent their summers in the 18th century; they would still feel at home. Although the property is only 1.5 km from Levanto, the bustle of modern life is left behind as you wend your way up the hillside through the silver-tinged olive groves. The red and cream villa stands in a small sunny clearing, next to a pleasantly dilapidated private chapel, where mass is still said once a year, on All Soul's Day. The newly opened B&B rooms are in a small rough-hewn stone farmhouse 100 metres beyond the villa. Giancarlo lives here too; an enthusiastic traveller himself, he really does enjoy meeting his guests. The rooms are done up in an aristocratic country style in tune with the main house, with wood and wrought iron artfully arranged against a background of rich yellows and blues. The private entrance to your room takes you from idyllic countryside straight into the pages of a glossy 'stylish interiors' magazine. Giancarlo grows organic apricots, figs and vegetables and makes his own wine and olive oil. You can devour the fruit at breakfast, perhaps sitting in the garden.

Rooms: 5 + 2 Apt: 3 D, 2 Tr, all en suite. 2 Apt for 6.
Price: D L130,000-190,000; Tr L200,000-250,000. Apt (for 4) L850,000-1,200,000, Apt (for 6) L1,000,000-1,500,000 weekly.
Breakfast: Included for rooms.
Meals: Not available.
Closed: November- Easter excluding Christmas.

How to get there: On A12 Genova — Livorno motorway, exit at Carrodano Levanto, follow signs to Levanto. 11km before entering town, you arrive at junction signposting Agriturismo Villanova. Left towards Monterosso and Cinque Terre. After about 1.2km, you'll find small private road on right.

Map Ref No: 7

Stella Maris
Via Marconi 4
19015 Levanto SP

Tel: 0187 808 258
Fax: 0187 807 351
E-mail: renza@hotelstellamaris.it
web: www.hotelstellamaris.it

Sig.ra Renza Pagnini

An elegant building in warm red with a cream trim. The frescoed ceiling in the entrance is just a hint of what is to come: rooms throughout have frescoed or stuccoed ceilings, contemporary with the house (1870) and depicting the activities carried out in each when it was a private villa. So when you open your eyes in the morning you gaze up at something unique. In other respects the décor is classical in style. Renza, bubbly and enterprising, is knowledgeable and enthusiastic about the frescoes and much else. She loves having guests and does the cooking herself, including occasional special dinners with music in the garden. Breakfast is a generous buffet. You'll do best to park at the hotel's annexe (*dipendenza*) and forget about the car until you leave: from here you can explore the Cinque Terre, including Monterosso, on foot; the beach is only 100m away, and trains stop here for Genoa and Pisa. Renza's children no longer live in, but there is a dear, bouncy basset-hound to add to the family atmosphere. Ask for a room at the back if you mind being on an animated street, and try for the main house rather than the annexe.

Rooms: 8: 1 S, 3 D, 1 Tw, 2 Tr, 1 Q, all en suite.
Price: Half-board: S L190,000; D/Tw L170,000 p.p;
Tr 150,000; Q 130,000 p.p.
Breakfast: Included.
Meals: Dinner included.
Closed: November.

How to get there: In Levanto Via Marconi is a lane off Via Jacopo da Levanto. The hotel is above the Carrige bank. Entrance around corner, press the first floor doorbell.

Map Ref No: 7

Albergo Pasquale

Via Fegina 4
19016 Monterosso al Mare SP

Tel: 0187 817 550
Fax: 0187 817 056
E-mail: pasquale@pasini.com
web: www.pasini.com

Sig.ra Felicita Ratti

It is deceptively old-looking, built straight onto the rock face at the water's edge. Albergo Pasquale was built in 1964 but local regulations ensured that it blended into its more elderly surroundings. The façade appears to belong to two houses: one lemon yellow and the other deep red with lemon trim. Before you get too excited, do you mind trains? They pass rather close and you may need to keep the windows closed. This is possible as all rooms are air-conditioned. Felicita, who runs this popular hotel with her son Marco, chats happily in English. Along the corridors, the rock has been left exposed as a feature and behind the bar is a 300-year-old watermill once used for grinding olives. The channels which brought the water to the mill are simply concreted up but only one bathroom grows the odd bit of mould. The main part of the village is closed to traffic after 10am so cars must be left at the beach car park 700 metres away. This may not be the right hotel if it is peace you are seeking, but it is in a spectacular position and you will be very well looked after. Felicita's cooking, by the way, is regional — and delicious.

Rooms: 15: 3 S, 12 D/Tw, all en suite.
Price: S L130,000, D/Tw L200,000.
Breakfast: Included.
Meals: Lunch and dinner available à la carte.
Closed: Never.

How to get there: Exit A12 at Carrodano-Levanto and follow signs for Levanto and Monterosso al Mare. After Levanto continue up towards Monterosso, pass through tunnel and straight on till right turn for Monterosso-Fegina. The road winds downhill for approx 5km to the town. At the bottom of the hill you can park in large car park (L10,000 per day).

Map Ref No: 7

Hotel Villa Steno

Via Roma 109
19016 Monterosso al Mare SP

Tel: 0187 817 028
Fax: 0187 817 354
E-mail: steno@pasini.com
web: www.pasini.com

Sig. Matteo Pasini

The bougainvillaea-painted walls of the Villa Steno, peeping above the trees at the end of a lane overlooking Monterosso, are a relief after the row of unprepossessing modern flats. Watching other guests finishing breakfast, or simply admiring the Ligurian Sea below, will make you want to join them on the sunny terrace overlooking the garden. The white-walled bedrooms have touches of blue and you should get a fantastic view from your balcony; only three rooms miss out and two of these look onto the garden. Matteo took over the management of the Villa Steno from his father some five years ago, but Angelo is still very much involved... some mornings he bakes fresh rolls and focaccia for you. Otherwise, breakfast is a delicious choice of cereals, local bread, honey, yoghurt and cheese. Matteo will be happy to provide maps for walkers. A path through the terraced garden is a shortcut to the village and the various coastal and inland tracks through the rugged beauty of the Cinque Terre. People travelling light often come by train, and enjoy the 10-15 minute walk to the hotel. Monterosso itself is a small, active, fishing port.

Rooms: 16: 3 S, 10 D, 2 Tr, 1 Q, all en suite.
Price: S L130,000, D L200,000, Tr L240,000, Q L260,000.
Breakfast: Included.
Meals: Not available.
Closed: Never.

How to get there: Exit A12 at Carrodano-Levanto and follow signs for Levanto and Monterosso al Mare. After Levanto, continue up the hill towards Monterosso, passing through tunnel and ignoring signs for Monterosso-Fegina. After 5km immediately on entering town turn right, signed Villa Steno.

Map Ref No: 7

Ca' dei Duxi

Via C. Colombo 36   **Tel:** 0187 920 036
19017 Riomaggiore SP

Sig.ri Giorgio & Samuele Germano

A real find. As soon as you walk in, you are greeted by the beaming smiles of Giorgio and his son Samuele, in the quaint stone/brick cubby-hole which serves as reception area. This 18th-century house stands in the quiet main street of a little Riviera village, one of the Cinque Terre; its transformation from dilapidation to warm, stylish modernity is a success. Rooms are mainly big, with plain, good taste; some have ancient ceiling beams like ships' masts. The views get better the higher up you are — there are a *lot* of stairs. The apartment (specify Via Colombo 34) is the most accessible. Odd, charming quirks are kept: one bathroom is 1m x 5m, another is built into the rock, visible through a perspex screen. Giorgio's life is devoted to making people happy: he's active on the local council and really cares about tourists getting the best possible impression of Italy. Some Italian families love Ca' dei Duxi so much they come back year after year. Parking can be difficult, so come by train if you can, travel light, and enjoy getting around by bus and boat. It's at its best outside July and August.

Rooms: 7: 3 D, 3 Q, all en suite, 1 Apt.
Price: D L160,000; Apt L800,000-
1,000,000 per week (not avail. August).
Breakfast: Included with rooms.
Meals: Half-board available L110,000 p.p.
Closed: Never.

How to get there: In la Spezia follow
signs toward Riomaggiore and Manarola.
Once you arrive in Riomaggiore, follow the
main road to the car park or turn right at
the station park and walk through the tunnel and turn left at the end up the main
street, Via Colombo, the hotel is on the left.

Agriturismo Riomaggiore

Via Lorenzo dei Batte'
19017 Riomaggiore SP

Tel: 0187 936 448
Fax: 0187 936 448

Sig.ra Franca & Anna Bonanini

Cousins Anna and Franca Bonanini own a couple of properties in Riomaggiore and a farm at nearby Brugnate. The local area is exceptionally lovely and a UNESCO heritage site and there are coastal views as far as Corsica and Elba on a clear day. The two apartments here are let for short-stays at remarkably reasonable rates. These are simple and pleasant without any very great distinction of architecture or style, though one house is easily spotted by its striking yellow shutters. Rooms vary; one overlooks the main street and is very sunny, the other is darker. Another, on the third floor up some very steep steps, may be unsuitable for families with young children or anyone not particularly spry. Both apartments have woodburning stoves, but neither has laundry facilities. Olives and grapes are grown here at Riomaggiore and open-air painting courses and cookery demonstrations are available. Franca's farming husband lives in the agriturismo at Brugnate — although not inspected, we know that it produces fruit, cereals, olive oil, wines and chestnuts and offers rather more in the way of rural charm.

Rooms: 5 + 2 Apt: 3 D, 1 Tr, 1 Q, all en suite. 2 Apt for 2-4.
Price: B&B: L50,000-60,000 p.p.
Half-board: L80,000-100,000 p.p.
Apt: L50,000-60,000 p.p.
Breakfast: Included with rooms.
Meals: Lunch L30,000; Dinner L30,000 on request.
Closed: Never.

How to get there: From La Spezia take the coastal route towards Levanto. Riomaggiore is closed to traffic so cars must be left in one of the two car parks. Arrangements should be made when booking to meet owners who will take you down to the house.

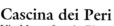

Cascina dei Peri

Via Montefrancio 71
19030 Castelnuovo Magra SP

Tel: 0187 674 085
Fax: 0187 674 085

Sig.ra Maria Angiola

The road rises through beautiful scenery to 100m above sea level and you come to a gate in a dauntingly high fence, where you ring and wait to be admitted. A charming garden awaits you, surrounding a farmhouse which is much more like a country villa. This is a full working farm with fields, poultry, vineyards and olive groves, which Signor Marcoli will be delighted to show you — commentary in Italian only! In the house the accent is on cool efficiency, echoed in the rather functional décor. A big plus is that Maria Angiola can mix B&B and half-board, so you can be spontaneous and flexible. It's a splendid centre in every way, with plenty of delightful walking which you can plan from the local maps up on the dining room walls. The beach and the promontory of Montemarcello are a short, pleasant drive away. Baby-sitting is available too. In low season two of the rooms can be joined to form an apartment. Rooms are of a good size and almost all have a sea view from their patio-terrace. It would be hard to be miserable here.

Rooms: 7: 3 D/Tw, 4 Q, all en suite.
Price: Half-board: L75,000-95,000 p.p.
Breakfast: Included.
Meals: Included.
Closed: Never.

How to get there: Exit A12 motorway at Sarzana take SS1 (Aurelia) towards Pisa for approx. 5km. Turn left for Castelnuovo Magra. Just before road begins to climb towards Castelnuovo turn left into Via Montefrancio. Continue along road for 1km where Agriturismo is signposted.

Map Ref No: 8

La Carnea

Via San Rocco 10
Carnea
19020 Follo SP

Tel: 0187 947 070

Sig. Ugo Fiechter

Ugo and Donata fled Milan 10 years ago and found their oasis in a stone farmhouse immersed in the wooded hills overlooking the Ligurian coast. Both are involved in environmental activities and their tiny two-hectare farm is organic. On the terraces are vines and olives dispersed among vegetables and fruit. The pantry shelves are lined with conserves, wine, oil and herb essences, all home produced. The bedrooms, in converted outbuildings, are simple and small and the bathrooms rudimentary, but the company is stimulating and the atmosphere relaxed. Donata loves to cook and the galleried dining room has glorious views over the valley down to the sea. Supper, usually vegetarian, isn't served until 9pm. and breakfast doesn't get underway until after 9am. La Carnea is an alternative way to enjoy the simple pleasures of life and from here you can walk the coastal route between the cliff towns along the Cinque Terre or trek in the nearby woods. There are no signs indicating La Carnea so have faith in the directions but there is a hint along the route — 'Siete quasi arrivati' ('You've almost arrived') — to assure you. *Not suitable for children.*

Rooms: 6: 3 D, 2 Tr, 1 Q, all en suite.
Price: B&B: L60,000 p.p. Half-board: L90,000 p.p.
Breakfast: Included.
Meals: Dinner L30,000 p.p.
Closed: February.

How to get there: Take the Vezzano Ligure exit off A12 motorway, take direction of Bottegna for 3km. Beyond Bottagna cross a bridge and turn left immediately after it for Valdurascathe. After 4km, right for Carnea, at the foot of the village take sharp turn into via S. Rocco. At chapel, turn right into a dirt road up (not down) through the woods for 1.5km. House at very top of the road.

Map Ref No: 8

Tuscany

"A man who has not been in Italy is always conscious of an
inferiority, from his not having seen what it is
expected a man should see."
Samuel Johnson

Fosdinovo Bed & Breakfast

Via Monte Carboli 12
54035 Fosdinovo MS

Tel: 0187 684 65
Fax: 0187 684 65
E-mail: rferraris@iol.it

Sig.ra Roberta Ferraris

Roberta and Ricardo have only just started doing B&B and seem to love it already. You can look at their 6,000 slides of Italy — Ricardo is a professional travel photographer — or browse through their library of books or their collections of rocks and shells. If you play the piano, or the guitar, you may get caught up in a lively music session. If not, you can settle down to listen to something from their vast collection of music. The open-plan living room leads onto a terrace and the view is spectacular. You are on a steep hill looking out onto a castle — floodlit at night — with la Spezia and the sea behind it and Elba in the distance. The two bedrooms are known as the *East* and *West* rooms and have hand-painted signs on the doors showing the sun rising or setting. The house is fresh and airy, with Roberta's watercolours on the walls. You could easily waste your stay in bed, for the rooms have inviting quilts and soft colours and Roberta makes sure there are always fresh flowers, fruit and chocolates — a charming and old fashioned touch that won't surprise you once you meet her.

Rooms: 2: 2 D, both en suite.
Price: S L65,000-85,000; D L90,000-120,000; Family L120,000-160,000.
Breakfast: Included.
Meals: Dinner on request menu L 40,000.
Closed: November.

How to get there: Exit A12 at Sarzana and follow SS1 for approx. 3km towards Carrara-Massa. Left onto SS446 towards Fosdinovo. Pass village and castle, turn right at x-roads towards Carrara. Left after 150m into Via Montecarboli, continue along bendy road for 400m and right onto a dirt road. The house is on the left.

Map Ref No: 8

Poderino Lero

Via In Campo 42   **Tel:** 0572 602 18
51010 Massa e Cozzile PT

Sig.ra Maria Luisa Nesti

This is the place for an 'alternative' break. Maria Luisa and Lucia offer courses in shiatsu, yoga or self-defence and Poderino Lero is a great place to meditate or simply unwind. Lucia is a therapist who runs self-discovery classes nearby, specialising in boosting the immune system and relieving stress and anger (so you can risk a marital row en route). Built against a hill in the early 19th century, with an old lemon tree over the door, the house is cool in summer and warm in winter and is surrounded by olives and vines which tumble down the hill. The large attic has been turned into a haven for meditation and yoga. The three bedrooms, large and furnished with country antiques, look clean but lived-in, with attractive fireplaces and a faint smell of pot pourri and herbs. Downstairs you will find Il Cantinone, a large open-plan room with a fireplace and comfy sofas and which opens onto the garden. Small pieces of Lucia's artwork are incorporated into the masonry. Maria Luisa is a sports enthusiast and the hands-on person at the Poderino. She will give you a home-made breakfast and suggest some restaurants a 10-minute drive away.

Rooms: 3: 2 D, 1 Tr, all en suite.
Price: S L70,000; D L100,000;
Tr L140,000.
Breakfast: Included.
Meals: Not available.
Closed: Never.

How to get there: From Montecatini follow signs towards Lucca, take right turning towards Massa and Cozzile. Follow road past Massa to the end of Cozzile.
Turn left towards Confine di Cozzile, right opposite shrine and follow lane to house.

           Map Ref No: 8

Casa Palmira

Via Faentina 4/1
Loc. Feriolo
50030 Borgo S. Lorenzo FI

Tel: 055 840 9749
Fax: 055 840 9749

Sig.ra Maria Assunta Fiorini

Casa Palmira, named after a 90-year-old lady of noble extraction who is the 'character' in nearby Borgo San Lorenzo, is a medieval farm which once guarded the road from Florence to Mugello. Assunta and Stefano have expertly restored it; clearly both have a gift both with houses and with people. Stefano will take you round neighbouring villages in their van but you might prefer to hire a mountain bike, tucking one of Assunta's thoughtfully packed picnic baskets on the back. They also run cooking and painting courses. The only trouble is that Casa Palmira is so welcoming, with its blend of old tiles, wooden floors and little touches like the door names cross-stitched by Assunta's sister, that you may not see much of this beautiful region: Florence is only 10 miles away and the Etruscan-Roman town of Fiesole only five. The bedrooms open off an unusual landing with a brick walled 'garden' in the centre — all Stefano's work. They look out onto the gardens, where Assunta grows herbs and vegetables, or onto vines and olive trees. There are plenty of restaurants nearby, but you really should try dinner 'at home'.

Rooms: 7 + 1 Apt: 4 D/Tw and 1 Tr, all en suite, 2 D/Tw sharing bathroom. 1 Apt for 2/4.
Price: S L80,000; D L110,000-145,000; Apt L750,000 (weekly).
Breakfast: Included.
Meals: Dinner, L35,000-L40,000, on request.
Closed: January & February.

How to get there: From Fiesole follow signs to Olmo. After 9km take the SS302 for Borgo S. Lorenzo. After approx. 2km turn right at signpost for Ristorante Feriolo, the house is on left.

Map Ref No: 8

Relais Chiara & Lorenzo

Via Casolari 74
Torri
50067 Rignano sull'Arno FI

Tel: 055 830 5240
Fax: 055 830 5240
E-mail: altox@centroin.it
web: www.pagineaffari.it/relais

Sig. Alberto Tozzi

There is a clutch of the ubiquitous white plastic garden furniture under the pergola, but the wooded views are gorgeous, the peace complete. You can see across the Arno to the outskirts of Florence, to the south is a castle and in the distance Vallombrosa glitters at night. From here you can 'do' most of Tuscany without exposing yourself to the rigours of modern urban sight-seeing. The 13th-century villa is lived-in and simply done, with large bedrooms sparsely but rather charmingly furnished: tiles, furniture with clean lines, white walls and painted shutters. There is a big fireplace in the living room and a Victorian-style bath with huge central, brass taps which sits in splendour in a spotless bathroom. The dining room is crisply modern, with more plain tiles, big pot plants in big white pots, delicately coloured walls... not your average 'Tuscan rustic'. The food here is delicious; some rate it as the best in the area. Alberto, happily retired from the rat race, is a "genial host", keen on the concept of bed and breakfast, English-style — he has the requisite coterie of country house dogs, too.

Rooms: 4: 3 Tw 1 private, 2 shared bath; 1 D/Tr en suite bath.
Price: Tw L120,000-140,000; D/Tr L150,000-170,000.
Breakfast: Included.
Meals: On request Lunch L25,000-35,000; Dinner L38,000 p.p.
Closed: Never.

How to get there: From Bagno a Ripoli or Pontassieve follow signs towards Rosano.
From Rosano continue to Volognano Torri. At approx. 1km turn left at signs to Relais Chiara e Lorenzo. The house is just over the brow of the hill at 800m.

Map Ref No: 9

Odina Agriturismo

Loc. Odina
52024 Loro Ciuffenna AR

Tel: 055 969 304
Fax: 055 969 305
E-mail: info@odina.it
web: www.odina.it

Sig.ra Alessandra Cerulli

The farmhouse is seven kilometres up a dusty unmade road, but from the top of the hill the view over the Arno Valley is fantastic. Alessandra, the manager, bubbles over with pride in Odina and you will see why when you get there; it's a marvellous pale-blue-shuttered house. The garden is newly planted, each bush and tree chosen with care, most being local species. The reception is in a beautifully restored, deconsecrated chapel, with a wonderful old bread-making chest. The apartments are all different, down to the work surfaces in the kitchen: some are granite, others the local *pietra serena*. Oil, vinegar, sugar, coffee, salt and washing-up liquid are provided in each kitchen and if you ask in advance they will lay in a store of basic supplies, though these you pay for. Each apartment has its own sitting area outside, with proper garden furniture rather than the ubiquitous white plastic. The pool is large, as are the bedrooms — all cream-coloured with oak beams and rustic antique furniture. If you don't want to cook, Alessandra will point you in the right direction.

Rooms: 4 Apt: 1 for 2, 2 for 5 and 1 for 6.
Price: L550,000-1,950,000 per week.
Breakfast: Self-catering.
Meals: Self-catering.
Closed: Never.

How to get there: In Florence take the A1 towards Rome. Exit at Valdarno. In Terranuova, follow signs towards Loro Ciuffenna, and before arriving into town turn left towards Querceto and Odina.

Agriturismo 'Il Leccio'

Via Case Sparse 35
50027 Strada in Chianti FI

Tel: 055 858 6103
Fax: 055 858 6106
web: www.emmeti.it/alleccio

Sig.ra Maria Luisa Landi

Any fan of Tuscany will recognise the name of this popular Chianti village. Il Leccio is a splendid tower house on the edge of the village in its own grounds. It's a building of great historic pedigree, begun in medieval times and restored by the present owners to its former glory. The interior frescoes and *trompe l'oeil* work are good enough to have caught the attention of art historians. The owners are titled folk and the house is really a 'stately home', but the Landis are delightfully down to earth. They happily cook, sew and run lace-making courses, besides welcoming people to their ancestral home with a refreshing lack of snobbery. All the rooms are doubles, with four-poster or canopied beds, and elegant drapes, dried flower displays, antiques etc. Most of the smartly tiled modern bathrooms have showers. Public rooms are huge and full of character. There's a vast baronial dining room with a chandelier, and a medieval-looking kitchen-diner where meat is roasted over an open fire. Staying here is an enormous pleasure, and excellent value; you can even get married in the family chapel.

Rooms: 10: 6 D/Tw, 4 Ste, all en suite.
Price: S L120,000-140,000; D L80,000-100,000; Ste L105,000-130,000.
Breakfast: Included.
Meals: Lunch L20,000. Dinner L50,000. Available on request.
Closed: 15 January-1 April.

How to get there: Via Case Sparse is at the top end of Strada in Chianti coming from the SS222 and is directly opposite the Restaurant Padellina. Follow the road a short way to the left around the school perimeter to their main driveway and car park.

64

Sovigliano

Strada Magliano 9
50028 Tavarnelle Val di Pesa FI

Tel: 055 807 6217
Fax: 055 805 0770
E-mail: sovigliano@ftbcc.it

Sig.ra Patrizia Bicego

Just outside the town down a country lane stands this ancient beamed Chianti farmhouse amid vineyards, olives, cypresses and pines. Though the setting is secluded and rural, it's in the heart of some of the most popular touring country in Italy, within sight (on a clear day, at least) of the towers of San Gimignano. Guests stay in self-catering apartments, one palatial with antiques and good, firm beds; or you may have one of the charming double rooms, with breakfast or dinner as well. A large communal kitchen-diner with a fireplace and a fridge for each bedroom makes a sociable place for guests to meet, but you can have your own space, too. There's plenty of sitting room and guests are free to help themselves to a pre-dinner drink. Besides the built-in attractions of this fine old house, what makes a stay here so special is the warmth and hospitality of the Bicego family, whose visitors, by all accounts, can scarcely bear to tear themselves away. Produce from the farm is on sale — *vin santo*, olive oil, grappa, etc — so come and decay gently.

Rooms: 4 + 3 Apt: 2 D, 2 Tw, all en suite; 3 Apt for 2-4.
Price: D/Tw L60,000-180,000; Apt. L170,000-370,000.
Breakfast: Included.
Meals: Dinner L45,000 on request.
Closed: Never.

How to get there: Exit SS Firenze-Siena at Tavarnelle. From town centre follow signs for Marcialla, Sovigliano is just out of town, turn left towards Marcialla down country lane signed Magliano, then follow signs for Sovigliano.

Map Ref No: 10

65

Fattoria Casa Sola
Via Cortine 88   **Tel:** 055 807 5028
50021 Barberino Val d'Elsa FI

Conte Giuseppe Gambaro

Count Giuseppe Gambaro and his wife Claudia tend the wine and olive oil production in person, as the family — originally from Genoa — has done for generations. The self-catering apartments are 700 metres from the main house and sleep from two to eight people. They are each on two floors with whitewashed walls, tiled floors, old wooden furniture and country cotton bedspreads. The Gambaros are aristocratic but down-to-earth, so this casually elegant look no doubt came naturally. Once a week the family takes guests round the vineyards and winemaking facilities, rounding off the visit with a glass of *vin santo* and *cantucci* (hard biscuits). The estate grows a variety of grapes: Sangiovese being the main ingredient of Casa Sola's prized Chianti Classico. They also run cookery and watercolour classes. Tennis and riding are only a couple of kilometres away and the swimming pool by the house is worth the walk — you suddenly come across it in the olive groves. You can cook in the apartments but why bother? Barberino and San Donato have several restaurants and Casa Sola is only 30-minutes drive from Florence and Siena.

Rooms: 3 Apt: 1 for 2, 1 for 6 and 1 for 8.
Price: Apt from L950,000-1,050,000
(Minimum stay 1 week in high season).
Breakfast: Self-catering.
Meals: Self-catering.
Closed: Never.

How to get there: From Firenze-Siena
superstrada exit in Florence at San Donato.
Follow SS101 past the church of San
Donato and turn right after about 1.5km
to Cortine and Casa Sola.

Villa Anna Maria
Strada Statale dell'Abetone 146
56010 Molina di Quosa PI

Tel: 050 850 139
Fax: 050 850 139

Sig. Claudio Zeppi

A place that feels like home even in winter; perfect if you are a video enthusiast — there are 3,000 of them. But 'real' Italy intrudes in grand measure: there is a shady tropical paradise of a garden to seduce the most world-weary urban cynic, a swimming pool soon to be built among the bamboo, woodland behind the house with a generous supply of easy-to-follow paths. It is an intriguing place, very laid back and easy — even bizarre — but with the confidence of a villa that has bedrooms untouched since the 17th century. The entrance hall is suitably huge, there is a games rooms with billiards and chess etc, and a library — all a touch over the top, perhaps, but very much in tune with the house and its slightly eccentric, hugely hospitable owners. They have no rules — virtually anything goes. They really do care more about people than they do about money. You can do your own breakfast if you wish, and the rooms that are your B&B homes can also be let as self-catering. Come with the same open minds as your hosts' and you will have a wonderful time.

Rooms: 6 + 2 Apt: 6 D, all en suite.
1 Apt for 2 and 1 Apt for 4.
Price: S L100,000; D L130,000;
Tr L180,000. Apt (for 2) L1,000,000;
Apt (for 4) L1,200,000 weekly .
Breakfast: Included.
Meals: Dinner, L40,000, on request.
Closed: Never.

How to get there: From Pisa take SS12
towards Lucca. At S.Giuliano Terme turn
left continuing down hill on SS12. After Rigoli continue to Molina di Quosa. Villa
Anna Maria is on the right opposite the pharmacy in Molina di Quosa.

Map Ref No: 8

La Locanda
Loc. Montanino
53017 Radda in Chianti SI

Tel: 0577 738 833
Fax: 0577 738 833
E-mail: info@la locanda.it
web: www.lalocanda.it

**Sig.ri Guido & Martina
Bevilaqua**

La Locanda appears to be just another Tuscan farmhouse, irregular thick stone walls with the traditional mottled terracotta roofs. But passing through the two buildings is like entering Alice's magic garden. A soft green lawn edged with Mediterranean shrubs gently slopes down to a pool; a covered terrace sits to the side overlooking Volpaia. Inside, the house throbs with bold colours and lively fabrics. The sunny living room with open fireplace and generous sofas reveals photos of Guido and Martina, he from the south and she from the north. They came here to set up their own little inn, scoured Tuscany for almost a year before finding the perfect spot. Courage and patience prevailed and in just over three years they have achieved miracles and renovated the two houses and decorated with fine antique pieces, prints, candles and a little library with books in various languages. The seven bedrooms are in a separate building and are generous in every way with large double beds and beautiful bathrooms. Martina cooks while Guido hosts; he makes wicked cocktails. Once settled in you'll find it hard to stir.

Rooms: 7: 4 D, 2 Tw, 1 Ste, all en suite.
Price: Tw/D L300,000-350,000; Ste L200,000 (single occupancy L250,000-300,000).
Breakfast: Included.
Meals: Dinner on request L50,000. excluding wine.
Closed: Mid-January — mid-March.

How to get there: From the village square of Volpaia, take the narrow road to the right which continues into a dirt road. Follow for approx. 3.5km reaching a small wooden sign marked 'La Locanda' to the left. Continue for a further 1km to the group of houses.

Map Ref No: 10

Borgo Casa Al Vento

Loc. Casa al Vento
53013 Gaiole in Chianti SI

Tel: 0577 749 068
Fax: 02 264 0754
E-mail: gioffry@tin.it
web: web.tin.it/ariete/

Sig. Giuseppe Giofereda

After the stunning approach road you may be disconcerted by the Casa al Vento's initially unprepossessing appearance, with its limp flags and mild untidiness; however, proceed undaunted to your airy rooms and prepare to unwind in this marvellously peaceful rural retreat, surrounded by green wooded hills, tree-fringed lake, olive groves and sunlit vineyards. Medieval in origin, the property was given a make-over five years ago, wood-beamed ceilings and red-tiled floors creating a rustic mood. Some of the bedroom décor is dodgy with a certain amount of dralon, nylon and velour; just ignore it and enjoy the views, breathe the wonderful air and look forward to sleeping like a baby. The owners are seldom in evidence but the obliging Sri Lankan custodians will see to your every need and do their best to make you feel comfortable. Sun terrace, garden, pool, tennis court (extra charge) and mountain bikes (ditto) are all on the spot, there's excellent walking all round, and historical and cultural visits are two-a-penny. If you go in the winter there'll be roaring wood fires.

Rooms: 12 Apts: 5 for 2, 1 for 3, 3 for 4, 1 for 5, 2 for 6.
Price: Apt. L400,000-3,000,000 weekly.
Breakfast: L10,000.
Meals: Dinner on request L30,000.
Closed: Never.

How to get there: On Siena side of Gaiole, take turning for Barbischio. House is 1.5km past Tower of Barbischio, well signposted from main road.

Locanda del Mulino

Loc. Mulino delle Bagnaie   **Tel:** 0577 747 103
53013 Gaiole in Chianti SI

Sig. G. Ceccarelli

Even the nuns of nearby San Giusto were once involved in a wrangle about Il Mulino — in 1221. Such key places were often fought over, and today who wouldn't give an arm to live beside a sweetly gurgling river in Tuscany? Only the birdsong will disturb your calm. Giorgio and his wife share a passion for good food and wine and are both excellent cooks. They originally ran Il Mulino as a restaurant, still with the old water-wheel and granite millstone. But its popularity made the Locanda (inn) inevitable. They have restored it all in honest sensitivity to the origins of the buildings, in simple Tuscan style, though the rooms are not ancient like the mill. Dinner is served on the terrace in warm months, and there is a large, shaded, and slightly unkempt garden into which you may retreat for a siesta. Keep your expectations low and you will be happy here, for it is as honest and decent as can be: thick stone walls, a lush valley, trees everywhere, and all so close to the vast museum of culture that is Tuscany.

Rooms: 5 D, all en suite.
Price: S L80,000; D L100,000.
Breakfast: Included.
Meals: À la carte menu available.
Closed: 1 November-1 March.

How to get there: From Siena, follow signs to Arezzo and Perugia. After about 9km, left towards Gaiole in Chianti. After about 5km right towards Gaiole in Chianti in Pianella proceed along country lane for about 3km, then left into white road signposted Locanda del Mulino.

Locanda 'Le Piazze'

Loc. Le Piazze
53032 Castellina in Chianti SI

Tel: 0577 743 190
Fax: 0577 743 191

Sig.ra Maureen Skelly Bonini

Don't give up! The road seems to descend into vast and empty space, taking you perilously far from certainty, but you are eventually rewarded with an oasis of unexpected luxury, and vast views over open countryside. As usual, it's an old farmhouse — restored with an eye for design and furnishings by Ralph Lauren, whoever he may be. Most bedrooms are of average size but impeccable, and some are huge — with their own terraces. The bathrooms are opulent enough not to remind you of home. If you simply cannot get away from your work there are fax and secretarial services available, though you'd better check with your spouse first. There are great open fireplaces, terraces, a fine swimming pool with uninterrupted views, books to devour and corners of the garden to retreat to. It's definitely a hotel rather than a B&B, and there is a crisp efficiency about the place that makes it popular with German visitors. The restaurant, in a very modern and attractive conservatory, is hugely appealing. Not for those looking for chaotic family fun, but perfect for a touch of pampering far from the tanning crowds.

Rooms: 25: 8 D, 17 Ste, all en suite.
Price: D L280,000-320,000;
Ste L360,000-400,000.
Breakfast: Included.
Meals: Dinner L60,000.
Closed: November-Easter.

How to get there: At the Poggibonsi exit of the Siena Firenze road, pass under the bridge and follow signs for Monteriggioni. After the first junction the hotel is on your left.

Map Ref No: 10

71

Poggio all'Olmo
Via Petriolo 30
50022 Greve in Chianti FI

Tel: 055 853 755
Fax: 055 853 755
E-mail: info@poggioallolmo.it
web: www.poggioallolmo.it

Sig. Francesca Vanni

Vin santo, designed to bring you post-prandial mellowness, is produced on this 11-acre farm, along with proper wine, olive oil, and a sense of peace available only in such places. The views are good, too: vineyards and olive groves, inevitably, all on those soft, undulating hills near Greve in Chianti. Three generations of Vannis still toil on the farm, grandfather pottering in the kitchen garden to grow fat tomatoes for guests and reminiscing interestingly about his past. Antonio runs the farm, and Francesca — his daughter — looks after you. It is just for people like these that agriturismo was invented, for it brings crucial income to small farmers. They are keen to do it well, and are still enthusiastic. The old hay-barn has become two one-bedroom apartments, each with a living room, kitchen and bathroom. The lower of the two has an extra bed and its own patio. The farmhouse has the two double rooms and a cleverly miniscule kitchenette. The new furniture is in Tuscan style, just right for the house. Here you will have a gentle encounter at home with an open-hearted family; nothing fancy, just good, honest stuff — and perfect peace.

Rooms: 2 + 2 Apt: 2 D, both en suite.
2 Apt for 2.
Price: D L140000. Apt L180,000-
210,000.
Breakfast: L15,000.
Meals: Dinner L35,000 on request.
Closed: Never.

How to get there: From Greve in Chianti
take SS222 towards Panzano. At approx.
2km turn left towards Lamole, follow for a
further 5km. Poggio all'Olmo is situated
between Vignamaggio and Lamole and is
well signposted.

Map Ref No: 10

Il Casale del Cotone

59 Loc. Cellole
53037 San Gimignano SI

Tel: 0577 943 236
E-mail: info@casaledelcotone

Sig. Alessandro Martelli

What a relief it is to escape the tour buses and heaving crowds of San Gimignano. Of course it's a must on the itinerary, but a day trip is quite enough and, besides, the long distance views over the vineyards and centuries-old olive groves of the towering 'New York' of Tuscany are part of the magic, too. Il Casale del Cotone dates back to 1500 and it was here in the parish 'Cellole' that Puccini was inspired to compose *Suore Angelica*. You may well be inspired and enchanted in your own way in this lovely setting. The Martelli family over the last five years has restored the old stone main villa into a comfortable country house. There are six big double rooms furnished in traditional local style; those on the ground floor have a private terrace but the views from the floor above are more spectacular. Breakfast is served outside in the courtyard opposite the little chapel; and when it's cooler, in the hunting room. Just across the road is the old coach house *Rocca degli Olivi* which has also been restored to its former glory and once again hosts weary travellers on the well trodden route between San Gimignano and Certaldo.

Rooms: 10: 8 D, 2 Tr, all en suite.
Price: D L170,000-200,000;
Tr L230,000-260,000.
Breakfast: Included.
Meals: Snacks only.
Closed: Never.

How to get there: From S. Gimignano, follow signs for Certaldo. Il Casale del Cotone is approx. 3km on the left.

Venzano
Mazzolla   **Tel:** 0588 390 95
56048 Volterra PI

Donald Leevers

A pure and reliable spring has nourished this place since very ancient times. It was granted to the Augustinian order in the 10th century and remained in their tender hands for over 900 years. The complex of buildings incorporates part of a Romanesque chapel and has grown throughout the centuries to serve the farming community. Although Venzano is now privately-owned the main thrust is still agricultural, though now with gardening as the focus. For a decade Donald and friends have been creating a luscious garden in a series of terraces moving outwards from the Roman spring. Their inspiration has been the monastery's love of plants for their beauty and for their usefulness. There is, of course, a long tradition of Italian garden design, tempered here by a sense of humility when contemplating the beauty of the surrounding countryside. Parts of the rambling building have been converted into apartments, all with close contact with the garden. Facilities are simple, but the décor of the living space is as attractive as it is sparse. Come for utter peace in a less-known corner of Tuscany.

Rooms: 3 Apt: 2 for 2, 1 for 3.
Price: Apt L980,000-1,610,000 per week.
Breakfast: Self-catering.
Meals: Self-catering.
Closed: 30 November-31 March.

How to get there: From Volterra towards Colle Val d'Elsa along the SS68 for about 10km. Turn right for Mazzolla and follows signs for Venzano.

Map Ref No: 10

Podere Le Mezzelune
Via Mezzelune 126
57020 Bibbona LI

Tel: 0586 670 266
Fax: 0586 671 814
E-mail: mezzelune@pop.multinet.it
web: www.mezzelune.it

Sig.ri Luisa & Sergio Chiesa

What a delight it was to find this house in the north Maremma, a little off the beaten track. After a long and winding dirt road, you come to a large wood-panelled gate. Ring the bell and it will swing open to reveal a tree-lined drive and a glimpse of the house. Miele the Labrador will probably be the first to greet you with Luisa in hot pursuit. The Chiesas have turned their beautiful home into a delightful bed and breakfast, simply and sympathetically. Downstairs was once home to the animals; now a huge dining table dominates the room where old and new friends can gather. Later you can retreat to the open fire or pass through to the garden and open loggia. Luisa has her little kitchen here, where her breakfasts are produced with panache; she also conjures up light lunches and more robust suppers. Four bedrooms are upstairs, each at a corner of the house with its own terrace; the two front rooms look out to the sea, and the other towards Bogheri and Castagneto Caducci. If you want to stay longer Luisa and Sergio have a little apartment in an annexe. Do stay, they are delightful people.

Rooms: 4 + 1 Apt: 4 D, all en suite. Apt for 2/3.
Price: L190,000-L220,000. Apt L1,350,000 per week.
Breakfast: Included.
Meals: Available on request.
Closed: Never.

How to get there: Exit SS1 at La California and follow directions for Bibbona. Just before the village you will see signs for Il Mezzelune on the left. Follow for approx 2km which will bring you to the gate of the farm. Ring for entry.

Gallinaio

Strada del Gallinaio 5
53035 Monteriggioni SI

Tel: 0577 304 751
Fax: 0577 304 793
E-mail: gallinaio@biemmepro.it
web: www.gallinaio.it

Sig. Gerhard Berz

If you badly need to escape from the frenetic pace of our new century, Gallinaio could be the perfect retreat; retreat is the operative word — stays are for a minimum of a week. Here all is total immersion; you have the peace and quiet of the Tuscan country side in a genuinely easy and friendly atmosphere. The house is a wonderful example of the local style with a stone arch opening into a courtyard, perfect for outdoor eating. Steps go up and down, here and there; shuttered windows punctuate the stone façade. Painting and meditation workshops are held regularly and you are not only welcome but positively encouraged to join in the labours of love and work in the garden, fields and woods. The end of November is a glorious time to view and participate in the olive harvest. Eating is communal and vegetarian with organically-grown vegetables from the garden. Take time to walk through the woods and observe the flora and fauna of the Montagnola park nearby. The isolation is by no means total, for the walled medieval city of Monteriggioni is only five minutes away and the bustle and cultural feast that is Siena another ten.

Rooms: 11: 8 D, 3 Tr, all en suite.
Price: S L170,000 p.p.; D L120,000 p.p.
Breakfast: Included.
Meals: Dinner L40,000 Lunch & Dinner L50,000.
Closed: January.

How to get there: Exit superstrada Firenze-Siena at Monteriggioni. Pass entrance to Monteriggioni and continue towards Siena. Continue for 1km where Gallinaio is signposted to the right. Turn right and follow the track for 1.3km where you will find the farm.

Map Ref No: 10

Villa Fiorita

Viale Cavour 75
53100 Siena SI

Tel: 0577 448 77
web: www.wel.it/villafiorita

Sig.ra Lara Giacomelli

Wafts of nostalgia drift elegantly through this roomy villa on the northern side of Siena (Palio fans may note it's in the *contrada*, or district, of the porcupine). It's furnished in the Liberty style which was all the rage in Italy during the early part of the century, and has enough distinction to attract the attention of Florence's architecture students. Antiques and conversation pieces (an old washstand here, a sewing machine there) grace many of the rooms, fresh flowers are standard fixtures, and parquet or marble floors add a touch of class. Each room is named after flowers and marked with a prettily painted ceramic tile. A striking feature of the house is its wide wooden staircase, typical of the period. There's plenty of public space for relaxing or reading, further reminders of a more leisured era. Our inspector thought it would make a great setting for a '20s and '30s weekend. At any rate, it has bags of atmosphere and style. Breakfast can be served either in bedrooms or in the garden. Lara and Mario are an outgoing, unpretentious couple. They enjoy ballroom dancing.

Rooms: 7 D/Tw, all en suite.
Price: S L90,000-129,000; D/Tw L90,000-140,000.
Breakfast: Not available.
Meals: Not available.
Closed: Christmas.

How to get there: Exit Firenze-Siena superstrada at Siena Nord. Right towards 'Centro'. At roundabout take exit to the far left into Via Florentina. At the 3rd set of traffic lights right and right again for rear entrance.

Map Ref No: 10

La Grotta di Montecchino

Via Grossetana 87
S. Andrea a Montecchino
53010 Costalpino SI

Tel: 0577 394 250
Fax: 0577 394 256

Dott. Agostino Pecciarini

Vines, olive groves, cypresses... you know the scene. Then there's the "patchwork of cultivated fields of corn and brilliant sunflowers that carpet the clay slopes, tamed and tended by (*sic*) centuries of peasant wisdom". The brochure says it, and it is true. You really can see Siena in the distance. Why stay there in the city when there is this to escape to so easily... even by bus, of which there are lots. The Grotta is a 25-acre organic farm producing wine, olive oil and corn. The 'dental doctor' owners are frustrated farmers and live here — where they can get their teeth into real work — as much as they can manage. Their own farmhouse quarters are 400 yards away. The apartments, although simple, have some nice touches, such as antique furniture, stencil decorations, wood-burning stoves for spring and autumn. Simonetta loves baking (who doesn't, who does it?) and creates gorgeous tarts. Some of the paint peels, and some of the furniture is makeshift, but the overall impression is of a solid farmhouse converted in sound taste and a great alternative to throwing money at a noisy, frenetic city-centre hotel.

Rooms: 4 Apt: for 2-4.
Price: Apt (for 2) L100,000-130,000;
Apt (for 3) L170,000-1,000,000;
Apt (for 4) L200,000- 400,000.
Breakfast: Self-catering.
Meals: Self-catering.
Closed: 15-30 November.

How to get there: From Siena take SS73
to Roccastrada. At Costalpino turn towards
S. Rocco a Pilli and Grosseto. On reaching
S. Andrea 'Montecchino' is signposted on the left. Follow farm track for about
1km to the farmhouse.

Map Ref No: 10

Podere Palazzo a Merse
Loc. Palazzo a Merse
53010 S. Rocco a Pilli SI

Tel: 0577 342 063
Fax: 0577 345 118
E-mail: parrinifede@ftbcc.it

**Sig.ri Federica &
Andrea Parrini**

Federica and Andrea are in their 30s and look younger; he runs a gym in Rosia and loves biking, she is a surveyor and keen horserider. Both are bright, unaffected and happy to chat. They converted this old mill (the canal it stood on is no longer there), with the help of their families who are builders and all is well-ordered and immaculately clean. Modern tiled floors throughout, new windows and doors, and shades of northern Italy and Switzerland in the ceramic stove and stencil-work — some of it Federica's own. Home crafts are a hobby and it shows in many decorative touches. The double room has solid old furniture and a really firm mattress. The twin is a little smaller and simply traditional, although the china in the cabinet is English. Both overlook the driveway and there's some road noise, but this is good value so close to Siena. The shared shower room is thoroughly modern with sparkling blue and white tiling and plenty of space. There's also a perfectly well-equipped apartment. The Parrinis have great plans for the garden; already there are geraniums, citrus fruit trees and camellias in huge terracotta pots.

Rooms: 2 + 1 Apt: 1 D, 1 Tw, sharing bathroom. 1 Apt for 4.
Price: L55,000 p.p.
Breakfast: L10,000.
Meals: Not available.
Closed: Never.

How to get there: From SS223 Siena-Grosseto, exit for Orgia & Rosia. At 0.5km from the junction you will find Palazzo Merse on the left. The house is the first, pass through the side gate to the front of the house. Entrance is up the external staircase on the first floor.

Il Colombaio

Podere Il Colombaio, No 12
Torri
53010 Sovicille Siena

Tel: 0577 344 027
Fax: 0577 344 027
E-mail: ilcolombaio@tin.it
web: www.toscanaholiday.com

Daniele Buraggi & Barbara Viale

Arty, dramatic, vibrant — as soon as you walk in you see that creative minds have
been at work. Strong, warm reds and oranges, a bold blue mosaic-top table and a
massive Scandinavian-inspired stove built by Daniele, originally from Milan, who
also made most of the furniture and painted all the pictures. Barbara is Venetian and
a ceramicist and her work, too, is everywhere, although she spends more time these
days looking after their young son and guests. The whole place is a live-in modern
art gallery and the old bones of the house, the knotted timbers, pitted stone steps
and well-trodden tile floors, seem perfectly at home with the arrangement. There's
some stylish new marble and tiling, a handsome reclaimed oak floor and innovative
paint effects. Bedrooms are named after their art: *Lovers, Warriors, Apache*. They
have all the essentials, nothing cosy or frilly, and leafy views through ancient glass.
The land all around is forested, terraced and olive-groved and belonged to the once
500-strong monastery at Torri (it has a superb cloister — do go and look). Good
walks and bike trails, 15 minutes from Siena — perfect for the unconventional.

Rooms: 5 D/Tr, 2 with en suite bath, 2
with private bath and 1 sharing bathroom.
Price: S L95,000-115,000, D L135,000-
155,000, Tr L175,000-195,000.
Breakfast: Included.
Meals: Available nearby.
Closed: 31 October-31 March.

How to get there: From Siena take the
SS223 towards Grosseto. After 12km, right
towards Rosia & Sovicille. Left towards
Torri at the junction marked by a tall cypress. Follow the avenue up to the village,
before it ends take the first left onto an unpaved road. Il Colombaio signed after
50m.

Az. Ag. Montestigliano

Loc. Montestigliano
53010 Rosia SI

Tel: 0577 342 189
Fax: 0577 342 100
E-mail: montes@ftbcc.it

Sig. Massimo Donati & Susan Pennington

Go on — dream of that classic Tuscan estate... then wind up the white road from the Siena plain to this group of handsome terracotta and rose-pink buildings and the dream becomes reality. Susan has lived here for 10 years, and runs these apartments with friendly, relaxed efficiency. Choose between the grand old family house, the Villa Donati, with boars' heads and dilapidated oils in the entrance hall, family furniture and fabrics, and the rest of the apartments named after the Donati children. They range from the high-ceilinged, large-windowed Villa Massimo, where *vin santo* grapes were stored, to the almost cottagey Villa Louisa. All tiled and shuttered, some have open fires, some have temperamental wood-burning stoves, loggia and gardens. Great views of forest, olive groves and vines and of Siena's distant towers. On the practical side, kitchens and bathrooms are mostly up-to-date, with just the occasional '50s touch, and entirely functional without being swish. Shaded walks, two good-sized swimming pools. A terrific, atmospheric place.

Rooms: 1 villa + 10 Apt: 1 villa for 12; 10 Apt for 3-8.
Price: L770,000 - 4,375,000 per week.
Breakfast: L12,000 on request.
Meals: Dinner, L40,000 on request Tuesday & Friday only.
Closed: Never.

How to get there: From Siena take SS223 south. After 12km turn right for Rosia & Orgia. After 1.5km take the dirt road to the left at the junction for Brenna marked Montestigliano.

La Casa del Vescovo
Via degli Orti
53016 Murlo SI

Tel: 0577 447 91
E-mail: medianet@iol.it

Sig. Luciano Cicali

The strange limestone hills known as the *Crete* on Siena's south-eastern flanks make fascinating touring; try to be there as the shadows lengthen. The house stands on the edge of a tiny perched village (originally Etruscan). From a distance it looks like a modern home, but it's actually a former bishop's palace dating from the 1600s or even earlier, still part of the neighbouring church complex. One bedroom opens (precariously) onto a walkway to the top of the old castle walls. Inside, the house is light and airy. Walls have decorative flourishes in the shape of stencilled borders, and furnishings include a few older pieces among modern fittings. Upstairs, there's some useful working space with a desk on a landing — handy if you need to set up a computer at some stage during your stay. The whole house is generally let as a single, self-catering unit. A small terrace set with tables and shaded by vines gives some outdoor sitting space. The owner, Luciano Cicali, lives in Siena but likes the outdoor life (hiking, climbing etc). His profession is the teaching of disabled children, so he is by nature a patient soul.

Rooms: 1 Apt: for 2-4.
Price: L800,000-1,300,000.
Breakfast: Self-catering.
Meals: Self-catering.
Closed: Never.

How to get there: South of Siena take the Cassia SS2 signposted Buonconvento. Through Monteroni. Opposite Lucignano right towards Vescovado di Murlo. At Vescovado follow signs towards Castello di Murlo. Follow road for 1km; house is within walls.

82

Map Ref No: 10

Podere Belcaro

Tenuta di San Fabiano
Monteroni d'Arbia SI

Tel: 0577 373 206
Fax: 0577 373 206
E-mail: simonmennell@hotmail.com

Simon Mennell

Podere Belcaro isn't easy to find but, once you have, you immediately feel at ease. Simon, your host, has been coming here for years to his 'Italian family' but recently decided to take up the offer of a spare farmhouse to create a retreat. Restoration has been done with the utmost respect for the origins of the simple, Tuscan farmhouse. The large open-plan kitchen where meals are prepared and often served, leads into a small living room dominated by a huge fireplace. Art courses are run here on a very small and personal scale and recent pieces by resident artist Philip Graves-Morris lie around the hearth; old terracotta tiles with painted scenes inspired by the famous *palio* medieval horse race in Siena. A narrow stone staircase winds up to five double rooms and two shared, stupendous bathrooms, one with a claw-footed bathtub. There are artistic touches everywhere, in the lightly colour-washed walls, in the beautiful wall hangings and rich fabrics. During the summer the house spills outside into the garden where there is a small secluded pool. Belcaro is also perfect to rent as a whole for a family or group of friends.

Rooms: 5 D, sharing two bathrooms.
Price: Available on request.
Breakfast: Self-catering. Breakfast on request.
Meals: Self-catering. Dinner on request.
Closed: Never.

How to get there: From SS2 turn left at Monteroni d'Arbia for Asciano. Follow road for approx 2km and turn left for Tenuta San Fabiano. The farmhouse is the second on the left and is to the right and behind the house facing the road.

Map Ref No: 10

Casabianca

Loc. Casabianca
53041 Asciano SI

Tel: 0577 704 362
Fax: 0577 704 362
E-mail: casabianca@casabianca.it
web: www.casabianca.it

Sig.ra Simonetta Demarchi

No sign of a 'white house' here; instead a medieval hamlet that has been meticulously restored. Although in theory this is a farm there is really more the feel of a gentleman's country estate; Simonetta Demarchi has seen to all the detail. The padronal villa with its tiny chapel standing alongside now contains a four-star hotel, some of the rooms still with the original 18th-century wall decoration. The surrounding farm houses and buildings have been made into fully self-contained apartments, each bearing the name of a native flower or the origin of the building; the restaurant in the old wine cellars still has the original vats and press. Even though there are several houses, each has the feel of an individual cottage, with contrasting painted walls and skirting boards, colour co-ordinated with carefully chosen furnishings and prints. Many have small terraces or balconies looking over the 65-acre estate. There are wonderful walks in the surrounding countryside, bikes to explore further afield, and you can meander down to the lake to fish, relax beside the pool or hide away in the secluded cloister garden.

Rooms: 9 + 20 Apt: 3 D; 6 Ste, all en suite. 20 Apt for 2-4.
Price: D/Tw L 270,000. Ste L440,000-550,000. Apt L150,000-3,000,000 per week.
Breakfast: Included in room price. L25,000. for Apt.
Meals: Dinner L50,000-L60,000.
Closed: January-Easter.

How to get there: Exit A1 at Valdichiana. Follow signs for Sinalunga and subsequently for Asciano. Casabianca is approx. 6km on the left after Asciano.

Map Ref No: 11

Castello di Gargonza

Loc. Gargonza
52048 Monte San Savino AR

Tel: 0575 847 021
Fax: 0575 847 054
E-mail: gargonza@teta.it
web: www.gargonza.it

Conte Roberto Gucciardini

No doubt some predatory hotel group will have its eye on this heavenly place. But right now it remains as a private, uniquely Italian, marriage of the exquisitely ancient and the adequately modern. Seen from the air it is perfect, as if shaped by the gods to inspire Man to greater works. One architectural writer described Gargonza as "my personal inner village". The old wall, largely intact, presses the houses against each other. There is a castellated tower, a great octagonal well in the main square, and a heavy gate that lets the road slip out and tumble down the slope. There is a garden, an old olive press for general use, houses (now self-catering apartments) echoing the simplicity of their former inhabitants, and a pleasant enough restaurant just outside. A swimming pool shelters in an olive grove, the tower above and the cypress-clad panorama below. You can choose to be in an apartment, or in the small, modest, hotel; wherever you are you can quietly allow this century to slip away. The walking and biking is as exhilarating as the thickly wooded countryside. The owner is passionate about restoring the village sensitively, slowly.

Rooms: 7 + 20 Apt: 2 D, 5 Ste, all en suite. 20 Apt for 2-10.
Price: S L145,000-165,000; D L175,000-195,000; Ste L260,000-280,000. Apt L840,000-2,695,000 weekly.
Breakfast: Included for rooms.
Meals: Restaurant 'La Torre di Gargonza' à la carte.
Closed: November & January.

How to get there: Exit A1 at Monte S. Savino. Follow SS73 towards Siena, at approx 11km after Monte S. Savino turn right towards Gargonza, then follow signs to Castello di Gargonza.

Dionora

Via Vicinale di Poggiano
53045 Montepulciano SI

Tel: 0578 717 496
Fax: 0578 717 498
E-mail: info@dionora.it
web: www.dionora.it

Sig.ra Cynthia Falconi

There's a long cypress-lined avenue to the isolated farm house. The vast views stir the soul, soft undulating hills and woodlands are punctuated by the occasional farmstead in cultivated fields of sunflowers, crops and olive groves. There are marked trails for walking and cycling. The thick stone walls of the old farmhouse act as a self-regulating thermostat giving respite from the arid heat in the summer and the bitter winds of the winter. The lounge with its vaulted tiled ceiling and washed walls displays old black and white photographs. Three rooms are in the main house where the owners live and a further three slightly smaller rooms are in the converted stable. Colours are warm and natural; four of the rooms have fireplaces and each has a luxurious bathroom complete with sauna and hydromasssage. Breakfast is served in the light and airy lemon house whose large glazed and arched windows welcome in the low, morning sun and frame the Tuscan landscape beyond the garden which slopes down to the swimming pool. A touch of luxury — Who can resist?

Rooms: 6 D with en suite bathroom, jacuzzi & sauna.
Price: L350,000-480,000.
Breakfast: Included.
Meals: Not available.
Closed: 15 January-15 February.

How to get there: From Montepulciano take SS146 to Pienza. After 1.5km left towards Poggiano and Dionora. Continue on dirt road for 1.5km and turn left into cypress-lined driveway to Dionora.

Map Ref No: 11

Castello di Ripa D'Orcia
Via della Contea1/16
53027 Ripa d'Orcia SI

Tel: 0577 897 376
Fax: 0577 898 038
E-mail: info@castelloripadorcia.com
web: www.castelloripadorcia.com

Famiglia Aluffi Pentini Rossi

One can only stand in awe. Ripa d'Orcia dates from the 13th century and was one of Siena's most important strongholds. The battlemented fortress (closed to the public) dominates the little *borgo* encircled by small medieval dwellings; apparently Saint Catherine of Siena took refuge here in 1377. The Aluffi Pentini Rossi family are descendants of the Piccolomini family who acquired the estate in 1484. The castle is their home and heritage of which they are hugely proud and one feels privileged to share it. All the rooms and apartments are big and simple but warm and welcoming, too, many with breathtaking views of the surrounding countryside. There is also a day room for guests, filled with family heirlooms and antique furniture and books to pour over. Breakfast is served in a small annexe off the main restaurant, open only in the evening, which serves good regional dishes. Ripa d'Orcia is a paradise for walkers, nature lovers and those looking for a complete escape. It is the silence, the scenery, the simplicity and the buildings themselves that are special.

Rooms: 6 + 7 Apt: 6 D/Tw, all en suite; 7 Apt.
Price: D/Tw L165,000-L190,000 per day. Apt L850,000-L1,280,000 per week.
Breakfast: Included.
Meals: À la carte menu available.
Closed: 1 November-1 March.

How to get there: From SS2 follow signs to San Quirico d'Orcia. Right over bridge and follow road around town walls for 700m. Right again (signposted Castello di Ripa d'Orcia) and continue for 5.3km to the castle.

Map Ref No: 11

Hotel Terme San Filippo

Via San Filippo 23
53020 San Filippo SI

Tel: 0577 872 982
Fax: 0577 872 684
E-mail: termesfilippo@tin.it

Sig.ra Anna Maria Maffeo

If you need a thermal cure, where better than the gorgeous Orcia valley? Slap on some mud, too. People come from all sorts of places to test for themselves the healing powers of the (some believe) miraculous minerals and you get occasional wafts of sulphur. There is a magnificent swimming pool, simple but thoroughly adequate hotel rooms and a slightly institutional dining room. You are reminded of a health farm when you see lots of your fellow guests wandering about unselfconsciously in dressing gowns. The atmosphere is serene, maybe even subdued, and there are no end of treatments and massages on offer to further subdue any remaining frenzy. Some of the treatments require a doctor's certificate and there is a medic on site. This is not the place to find the sort of Tuscan interiors you might expect from this book, but you'll be perfectly comfortable, so why not try a new form of self-indulgence? Just up the hill is the old Roman open-air thermal pool, the centrepiece of the tiny hamlet that attracts many visitors.

Rooms: 27: 4 S, 23 D, all en suite.
Price: B&B: S L90,000-100,000;
D L150,000-180,000. Half-board:
L95,000-115,000 p.p. Full-board:
L105,000-125,000 p.p.
Breakfast: Included.
Meals: Lunch L30,000; Dinner L35,000.
Closed: December-April.

How to get there: From SS2 towards
Rome follow signs towards Bagni S.Filippo.
Via S. Filippo is the main road in the
village.

Map Ref No: 11

Sette Querce
Viale Manciati 2-5
53040 San Casciano dei Bagni SI

Tel: 0578 581 74
Fax: 0578 581 72
web: www.evols.it/settequerce

Sig. Guglielmo Mei

Just off the main road in San Casciano dei Bagni an innocent looking three-story house is just about ready to burst at the seams, a riot of colour from floor to ceiling, earthy tones on the ground floor to starling blues on the top. This old three-storey country inn, recently revamped and given a new lease of life, vibrates with energy. There are nine suites, some of which have terraces and all of which have a cosy seating area, some with open fireplaces. Each has its own very personal style and character, bold tones, strongly contrasting fabrics, throws and mats, all mixed and matched, highlighted by soft lighting and punctuated by old photographs and architectural prints. Each piece has been deliberately studied, chosen and placed. These rooms are not for the weak hearted. Across the main square in the old stables is the restaurant *Daniela*, a little more sombre in contrast, with exposed brick walls and simple untreated wooden tables and chairs. Nearby is Fonteverde Spa where you can enjoy the thermal waters. Sette Querce is fun and lively and a refreshing break from the norm.

Rooms: 9 Ste, all en suite.
Price: L270,000-380,000.
Breakfast: Included.
Meals: À la carte menu available.
Closed: 15 days in January.

How to get there: Follow the SS321 to San Casciano dei Bagni. The hotel is on the left just before entering the old centre; follow road for 300m.

La Crocetta

Loc. La Crocetta
53040 San Casciano dei Bagni SI

Tel: 0578 583 60
Fax: 0578 583 53

Sig.ri Andrea & Cristina Leotti

This 900-acre estate spills over with the good things in life: timber, cereals, wine and olive oil. The large stone building dates from 1835, and was completely restored in 1993. Though only five minutes from town and next to a main road, it is shielded by oak trees and a large garden and feels completely secluded. The interior is traditionally furnished in a rather English style with attractively colourwashed or stencilled walls, rush-seat chairs and matching chintzy fabrics. Open fires and exposed beams add extra warmth to the place. Bedrooms are simple but cosy, with good modern shower rooms. Most have double-aspect windows and unfussy canopied beds. Cooking is a strong point and mouth-watering smells drift in from the spotless kitchen towards mealtimes. There's always a good choice, including a veggie option. Cristina and Andrea are equally engaging and you'll find conversation with both easy. They are helpful, too, with wide-ranging interests; he's the cook, while she is keen on interior decorating. Anyone allergic to cats should be aware that there were 10 around at the last count.

Rooms: 8: 1 S, 5 D, 2 Tw, all en suite.
Price: S L77,500; D/Tw L155,000. Children half-price.
Breakfast: Included.
Meals: Lunch/ Dinner à la carte.
Closed: Mid-November — mid-March.

How to get there: Exit A1 at the Chiusi and follow signs for S. Casciano dei Bagni.

Map Ref No: 11

Le Radici Natura & Benessere

Loc. Palazzone
53040 San Casciano dei Bagni SI

Tel: 0578 560 38
Fax: 0578 560 33
E-mail: radici@ftbcc.it

Sig.ri Alfredo Ferrari and Marcello Mancini

The densely wooded unmade road that leads to Le Radici gives little away. It twists and curves and just when you think you'll never make it, opens into a little oasis. For Alfredo and Marcello the conversion of this solitary 15th-century stone farmhouse has been a labour of love. Alfredo scoured the antique markets and raided his stock of family heirlooms to furnish the 10 rooms that they have decorated in a refined country style. They are a generous size, the delicately toned hand-finished walls punctuated with colour in bold, upholstered pieces and kilim rugs. Alfredo has been able to indulge his passion for cooking with the small restaurant they have created in the vaulted former sty, and revels in the easy availability of Tuscany's famous ingredients. The geraniums revel in the micro-climate and bloom even in November, tumbling down from large urns, window sills and balconies. A beautiful pool blends into the landscape and a little winding foot path takes you up to the wooded crown of the hill where you can sit and enjoy the glorious views.

Rooms: 10: 7 D, 3 Ste, all en suite.
Price: D L170,000-200,000;
Ste L250,000-300,000.
Breakfast: Included.
Meals: Lunch/Dinner available on request, L50,000 excluding wine.
Closed: Never.

How to get there: From A1 exit at Chuisi and follow signs for S. Casciano & Palazzone. Turn right for Palazzone. Pass directly through village and continue onto unmade road, the road winds up steeply for approx. 3km, passing a small church on the right. Le Radici is signposted down a narrower track to the left.

Map Ref No: 11

Villa Iris

Strada Palazzo di Piero 1
53047 Sarteano SI

Tel: 0578 265 993
E-mail: villairis@ftbcc.it

Dott. Fabio Moretto

The Moretto family escaped Milan to retreat here to the Tuscan hills two years ago. Bed and breakfast seemed an obvious choice; both are well travelled, bilingual and sociable hosts. Fabio is Italian and Hashimoto is Japanese; her influence has given the house an unusual blend of Eastern and Western design, even though the oldest parts of the farmhouse are 16th century. In the day room are a reading corner and grand piano which they love to play. Hashimoto also paints porcelain; her delicate pieces are placed around the house. The five bedrooms, big and filled with light and space, have been thought out with the greatest attention to detail. In the bathrooms they have used the local apricot marble for the floors and splash-backs, and soft towels add a touch of luxury. A leisurely breakfast of Tuscan delicacies, such as local hams, salami, honey and bread, is served in the glass conservatory; even in the cooler months you can feel that you are dining *al fresco*. During the day you can doze in the garden, cool off in the pool, or explore the archaeological treasures of ancient Etruria.

Rooms: 5: 1 S, 3 D, 1 Ste, all en suite.
Price: S L120,000-150,000; D L200,000-250,000; Ste L250,000-300,000.
Breakfast: Included.
Meals: Not available.
Closed: November 1-31 March.

How to get there: Exit A1 at Chuisi-Chianciano Terme. Take SS46 towards Chianciano Terme. After approx. 4km left at blue signpost to 'Villa Iris'. Follow for 400m and turn right down unpaved road for 700 m. Villa Iris is on left; the gate is electric so ring.

Map Ref No: 11

La Palazzina

Sant' Andrea di Sorbello
52040 Mercatale di Cortona AR

Tel: 0575 638 111
Fax: 0575 638 111
E-mail: italianencounters@technet.it
web: www.italianencounters.com

David & Salina Lloyd-Edwards

Hannibal slaughtered the Roman army at nearby Lake Trasimeno and there is little that David doesn't know about the battle, and about Hannibal himself. Do let him bring it to life, for he is the most amiable and engaging of hosts, with a huge enthusiasm for his corner of Italy. There is, no doubt, an English inflection to La Palazzina, it is undeniably attractive, a quirky little 14th-century tower inexplicably planted alongside the main house. It belonged to the castle just up the hill and is now a self-contained retreat, easy to live in, comfortable, and with luscious views across the wooded valley. The top room has an attractive beehive ceiling, and all the rooms have that cosy roundness which makes sleep come easily. The terrace is just how you would hope it to be, with cypress trees marching sedately up the hill and nothing to disturb your serenity. Indeed, there are beautiful walks from the very door. There is an apartment in the main house, too, where David and Salina will give you dinner on your first evening, before you have found your gastronomic feet.

Rooms: 2 Apt: Tower for 4; Apt for 2.
Price: Tower L1,300,000-1,700,000 per week. Apt L150,000-180,000 per night. Minimum stay 3 nights.
Breakfast: Self-catering.
Meals: Self-catering. Dinner with wine, L30,000. Please order at time of booking.
Closed: Never.

How to get there: Directions will be given at time of booking.

Map Ref No: 11

Stoppiacce

San Pietro A Dame
52044 Cortona AR

Tel: 0575 690 058
Fax: 0575 690 058

2002 129 Euro/ night

Colin & Scarlett Campbell

Chestnuts were once put to dry in the tiny stone dwelling below the main house, hence the name — Il Castagno. It is as intimate and cosy a retreat as any couple could want, with its own terrace and wonderful views over the lushly wooded valley, itself no less peaceful than it has been for hundreds of years. The pool, higher up on the hill, has the sort of prettiness and views that make one's return home to face a long winter even less palatable than usual. The white walls, painted furniture, wooden beams and plain colours of the interior are perfect; no unnecessary frills to tarnish the simplicity. Stay here on a B&B basis or take it for a week. Breakfast by yourselves, or pop up to the main house, where there are three bedrooms, equally sensitively done up. Scarlett and Colin are English, immensely sociable and easy-going. Just do your own thing or dine with them if you like; Scarlett cooks too well for you not to. This is an isolated spot so don't imagine you can nip off to take in a church or two before breakfast.

Rooms: 3 + 1 Apt: 3 D, 1 with bath, 1 with shower. 1 Apt for 2.
Price: D L220,000. Apt L300,000, min 3 nights.
Breakfast: Included with rooms.
Meals: Lunch L45,000, Dinner L85,000 on request.
Closed: November-March.

How to get there: From Cortona follow signs to Citta di Castello for approx. 7km to Portole. Take left fork to San Pietro a Dame. Pass through village and after approx. 1km turn right at US mail box marked Stoppiacce, and continue down the dirt road.

Map Ref No: 11

Umbria

"Some people stay longer in an hour
than others can in a week."
William Dean Hotwells

Villa Pia
06010 Lippiano PG

Tel: 075 850 2027
Fax: 075 850 2127

Morag Cleland

Kevin and Morag make Villa Pia — a beautiful old *Casa Padronale* or manor house — a very special place for children. Both used to work with disadvantaged young people and have two young children of their own. They provide an early supper at six, to give you time to put your children to bed before dinner. This is eaten communally in the kitchen where you can watch Kevin at work; he used to be a chef at the Dorchester and with the superb, fresh ingredients on hand here he produces memorable meals. Breakfast awaits even those who stagger downstairs late. The bedrooms range from big to very big and most have decoratively painted ceilings. Apart from this, they are simple, with quiet colours and traditional furniture. One great thing about the house, which goes back to the 15th century, is that it looked very similar 100 years ago — except for the bathrooms. The children can explore the huge grounds while you lie by the pool, and a stone barn has been made into a childrens' play area. There's even baby-sitting available — so come here to be reminded that children matter in Italy.

Rooms: 12: 6 D/Tw, all en suite; 4 D/Tw with private bathrooms; 2 D/Tw sharing bathroom.
Price: Full-board: £399 p.p. April; £ 440 p.p. May-November (child £180) weekly.
Breakfast: Included.
Meals: Lunch & Dinner included except Thursday.
Closed: November-March.

How to get there: Take SS221 to Monterchi, circle town avoiding the centre. After a further 4km turn right for Lippiano. At the T-junction in village turn right and then left at the roundabout. The house is just behind the castle.

Locanda del Gallo
Loc. S. Cristina
06020 Gubbio PG

Tel: 075 922 9912
Fax: 075 922 9912
E-mail:
locanda.del.gallo@infoservice.it
web: www.locandadelgallo.it

Marchesi Paola Moro

Because Santa Cristina is in a pure medieval hamlet, with all the architectural features that one would expect — such as beamed ceilings and terracotta floors — it is awash with history and has the unmistakable feel of a colonial home. Rooms are light and airy, with pale coloured lime-wash walls which accentuate perfectly the rich brown hardwood furniture and oriental artefacts. The bedrooms have carved four-poster beds draped with fringed counterpanes. There is an air of calm and tranquility here, you are somehow deprived of your favourite worries and forced to relax. A narrow paved terrace wraps itself around the house; here you can doze in wicker armchairs or enjoy drinks at dusk as the sun melts into the Tiberina valley. The pool is spectacular, like a mirage clinging to the side of the hill. The *Gallo*, meaning cockerel in English is almost everywhere you look. According to Balinese tradition he wards off evil sprits. He is hard at work here. Other traditions are also upheld; healthy food rich in genuine flavours, cold pressed olive oil, aromatic herbs, vegetables from the garden, home baked bread and cakes...

Rooms: 7: 4 D, 3 Ste (2xD), all en suite.
Price: B&B: D L80,000; Ste L70,000. Half-board: L120,000 p.p.
Breakfast: Included.
Meals: Dinner available on half-board basis.
Closed: January & February.

How to get there: From Gubbio follow signs to Perugia. After approx. 8km right to S. Cristina and follow winding panoramic road for 10km. Turn right at sharp bend towards Locanda del Gallo.

Map Ref No: 11

Prato di Sotto

Santa Giuliana
06015 Pietrantonio PG

Tel: 075 941 7383
Fax: 075 941 7383
E-mail: penny@retein.net

Ms. Penny Radford Young

It is hard not to dream of living right here, in Prato di Sotto. It is lost in the rugged Umbrian countryside, perched on a hill overlooking the 12th-century village of Santa Giuliana. Penny and Harry, the English owners, have made each apartment feel like a home, one that might feature in a magazine. The kitchens have been designed for serious cooking after some serious shopping, although catering can be arranged on request. Casa Antica is the biggest apartment, with French windows leading onto a fig-shaded terrace from the main bedroom. La Terrazza has its own terrace, draped in vines and white roses. Il Molino, a 13th-century oil mill, is a romantic studio for two with a huge shady veranda, while the cottage, up by the swimming pool, is covered in flowers and has the best view of all. The floors are mellow terracotta with soft-coloured kilims, the walls white brick and the big, solid beds have the sort of crisp sheets you want to jump between. You can borrow a friendly Labrador, or three, for your rambles through the olive groves, or go for a sail in Penny and Harry's boat on Lake Trasimeno.

Rooms: 4 Apt: 4 for 2-5.
Price: Apt £400-800 per week.
Breakfast: Self-catering.
Meals: Self-catering.
Closed: Never.

How to get there: From Umbertide take No 3 bis south exiting at Badia Monte Corona. Under railway bridge and left at T-junction. Continue along main road, passing Badia Monte Corona, for 3km and take first left onto unmade road. Follow for a further 4km veering left on approach to Santa Giuliana. The house is the first on the right.

Map Ref No: 11

Castello di Montegualandro

Montegualandro 1   **Tel:** 075 823 0267
06069 Tuoro sul Trasimeno. PG   **Fax:** 075 823 0267

Sig. Claudio Marti

In a 15th-century painting of Montegualandro, the only difference from today's picture is the absence of the thick wall of trees. The castle's first known owner was Charlemagne, but it is said that Hannibal camped on this spot before his defeat at Lake Trasimeno, which the hill overlooks. Begun in the 12th century, Montegualandro was rebuilt in the 15th and, perched on the Tuscan-Umbrian border, was a prized possession in the wars between the Tuscan Granduchy and the Church. This is probably a place to come without the children, not that they are unwelcome. Restoration over the years has been careful to preserve traces of the past; a section of ancient floor has been covered in glass to preserve it intact. Rooms in the apartments — which have kept the character of their original function, such as kilns in the old bakery — are not large but they are peaceful and stylish, with whitewashed walls and antique furniture that looks at home. You need to drive a few miles to find the excellent local restaurants, but you will find plenty as you explore the area.

Rooms: 4 Apts: 3 for 3 and 1 for 4.
Price: L800,000-950,000 weekly.
10% discount for 2 week stay.
Breakfast: Self-catering.
Meals: Self-catering.
Closed: Never.

How to get there: Exit the Bettolle-Perugia superstrada at Tuoro sul Trasimeno, right towards the town. Then left at junction for Arezzo and follow road for 2.2km. Right at the 'Vino Olio' sign and follow dirt road uphill to the castle. Turn right before sign 'strada della caccia' and continue up to the iron bar.

Castello dell' Oscano

Strada della Forcella 37
06010 Cenerente PG

Tel: 075 584 371
Fax: 075 690 666
E-mail: info@oscano.com
web: www.oscano.com

Sig.ri Michele Ravano & Maurizio Bussolati

At the turn of the century Count Telfner visited England and was so taken by the opulent intimacy of its grand country houses that he couldn't wait to get back and do his own place. Hence Oscano today — a glorious, lovable parody of England, and irresistible. There is a grand balustraded central staircase and gallery, huge landscape paintings on most of the walls, a grand piano in the drawing room and a little library for afternoon tea. The sitting room would be at home in Kent. Maurizio has nurtured the house almost since its re-birth as a hotel. He returned from Belgium with a *faux trompe l'oeil*, commissioned ceramics from Deruta, stocked the cellars with the best of Umbria. The bedrooms are not a disappointment after all this: classical, antique-furnished, floral, wall-papered, with period furnishings and large windows over the garden and park. The rooms in the Villa Ada are not so stylish, but 'well appointed' — as they say, and hugely comfortable. The whole experience is of comfort, unpretentious refinement, utter peace. The food is excellent, to boot.

Rooms: 30 + 13 Apt: 20 D, 10 Ste, all en suite. 13 Apt for 2-5.
Price: D L240,000-320,000;
Tr L310,000-440,000; Ste L420,000;
Apt L600,000-1,080,000.
Breakfast: Included.
Meals: Dinner L60,000.
Closed: Never.

How to get there: Exit E45 Perugia Madonna. From Perugia follow signs for S. Marco and subsequently a small secondary road for Cenerente. From here Oscano is well marked.

Via Cupa 44

Collebaldo
06060 Castiglion Fosco PG

Tel: 075 835 5859
Fax: 075 835 5859

Michael Bishop

It's fun to stay in a village. You can enjoy all the local activity and festivities — the two Michaels know everyone and are perfect hosts. On their recent trip to England all the neighbours stood by to wave them off and then came by to greet them on their return... they only went for a week. Five years ago they stumbled upon this little terraced house and immediately fell in love with the view from the back towards the unusual open bell tower of the church across the valley and beyond to the rolling Umbrian hills. The house has two bedrooms which share a bathroom and they let which ever takes their fancy. At the back is a periwinkle blue double with views over the valley and at the front a twin with lively checked duvets to snuggle into and prime viewing of village events. Both Michaels are vegetarians, a rare find in Italy, and young Michael is more than willing to cook for you providing you are willing to accept what's on 'the menu'. There's lots to explore nearby, but do take time to relax, chat and enjoy a glass of wine with your hosts. They are a sound cultural alternative to all those galleries and churches.

Rooms: 1: 1 D/Tw, sharing bathroom.
Price: S L55,000; D L40,000 p.p.
Breakfast: Included.
Meals: Dinner L15,000-25,000.
Closed: Never.

How to get there: From Perugia take SS220 towards Citta di Pieve. At Tavernelle turn left for Oro & Collebaldo. Keep to the right for Collebaldo. At church in village turn left into Via Cupo. The house is second on right.

La Torre
Voc. Pitroso 70
06060 Pietrafitta PG

Tel: 075 839 127
Fax: 075 839 127

Simon Parks

If you have always dreamed of an etching holiday in Italy look no further. Use of the resident etching press is free — and encouraged. The apartments in the main house are usually let to artists, so there's often a welcome artistic presence at La Torre. The tower itself has a ground-floor kitchen-living area and bathroom. A spiral staircase leads directly to the main bedroom, with traditional chestnut doors leading to the external staircase. Above is a twin room, up a steep staircase and a showcase for locally-produced works of art. It is ideal for a small family looking for simplicity and utter peace. There's a swimming hole on the edge of the property, good for the friendlier among you — you may have to share it with the odd fish or frog — and a nature reserve borders one side of the property. Guests are welcome to help themselves to vegetables — organically grown — from the garden. Horse riding is available two kilometres away and you are a stone's throw from the voluptuous Lake Trasimeno. Simon — the manager here and an artist himself — is genuinely nice. *Weekly hire only.*

Rooms: 1 Apt: for 4.
Price: L720,000-L850,000 per week.
Breakfast: Self-catering.
Meals: Self-catering.
Closed: Never.

How to get there: From Perugia take the SS220 towards Citta della Pieve, after about 24km turn left towards Pietrafitta at foothill of Pietrafitta, turn right towards Fontana & Casaglia, left at fork and after 800m there is a large oak on the right, turn here and follow the dirt road to the house.

Map Ref No: 11

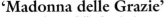

'Madonna delle Grazie'

Loc. Madonna delle Grazie 6
06062 Città della Pieve PG

Tel: 0578 299 822
Fax: 0578 299 822
E-mail: madgrazie@ftbcc.it

B&B - SS
£50 -SS

Sig. Renato Nannotti

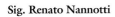

Children who love animals will be in heaven here. Renato will pluck a cicada from an olive tree and show them how it 'sings' and they can pet the rabbits, dogs and ducks — and even the chickens — to their hearts' content. Renato also has horses, which you can ride. Madonna delle Grazie is a real farm, not a hotel with a few animals wandering around, so don't expect any luxury; it is 'basic' at its best. However, the five rooms in the 18th-century farmhouse all have their own bathrooms and the food is delicious. The farm is fully organic; supper, which is eaten *en famille*, includes Renato's own salami, chicken, fruit and vegetables as well as the farm's olive oil, wine and even grappa — which he will be quick to give you if he thinks you need it. Apart from the animals, there is a big playground for the children and table football in the house, while (only!) the youngest will like the incongruous Disney figures (gnomes) dotted around the picnic area. For the grown-ups there is a discount at the spa at S. Casciano Terme. Perugia is only a short drive away, for an intensely satisfying immersion in culture.

Rooms: 5 D, all en suite.
Price: B&B: L70,000-90,000.
Half-board: L90,000-105,000 p.p.
Breakfast: Included.
Meals: Dinner always available, excluding wine, L20,000-25,000.
Closed: Never.

How to get there: From Chiusi follow signs south towards Città della Pieve. Just outside the town in the direction of Orvieto turn right towards Ponticello and proceed downhill for 1.5km. Madonna delle Grazie is on the left.

Villa Ciconia

Via dei Tigli 69
Loc. Ciconia
05019 Orvieto TR

Tel: 0763 305 582
Fax: 0763 302 077

Sig. Valentino Petrangeli

Industrial suburbs, a railway line, autostart junctions — not what you expect from Orvieto, one of Umbria's most fascinating hill-towns. The fine stone villa covered with flowers, however, is partly shielded from traffic noise by its large shady gardens. The house was begun in the 16th century; cavernous rooms ramble through the house, some rather austere, but all impressive. Two large dining rooms decked with tapestries and frescoes occupy much of the ground floor, their chilly proportions offset by huge fireplaces. The smaller breakfast room has a more intimate feel, with white walls and ancient tiled floors. The regional food is delicious, with specialities like porcini mushrooms. Bedrooms are mostly large and uncluttered, with plain white walls. Furnishings are simple, but some rooms have handsome old-fashioned wardrobes or canopied beds and iron bedsteads with the VC insignia. Two of the bathrooms have a Jacuzzi bath. Sig. Falcone gallantly runs the hotel almost single handedly but will always find time for you.

Rooms: 10 D/Tw, all en suite.
Price: B&B: S L210,000-260,000;
D/Tw L240,000-280,000.
Breakfast: Included.
Meals: Lunch/Dinner L35,000.
Closed: Never.

How to get there: Exit A1 at Orvieto.
From roundabout take SS71 towards
Arezzo. Villa Ciconia is situated at approx.
1km on left.

103

Map Ref No: 11

Relais Il Canalicchio
Via della Piazza 13
06050 Canalicchio di
Collazzone PG

Tel: 075 870 7325
Fax: 075 870 7296
E-mail: relais@ntt.it
web:
www.wel.it/Rcanalicchio.html

Sig. Orfeo Vassallo

Not only a diversion between Perugia and Orvieto and a convenient stop coming up north from Rome, but also a good retreat for a couple of days. Once known as the Castello di Poggio, this 13th-century hamlet in the lush green Umbrian countryside is almost a principality in itself; 23 rooms, a pool, gardens, gym and, of course, a tower — all within the fortress walls. The old olive mill still has the press and granite stones. Unconventionally, however, the decoration is an international mix, an oddity reflected in the various names of the rooms, such as *Isabelle Rubens* and *The Countess of Oxford*. The walls are striped and the bedcovers and drapes are floral. Some are tucked under the beamed eaves of the roof; many open onto little balconies. Perhaps those in the tower are the nicest: the views from the eight windows sweep in all directions over an endless valley of olive groves, vineyards and woods. Downstairs you can enjoy a frame of billiards and a glass of grappa, having dined in the splendid restaurant *Il Pavone*. The more sedate among you may retreat to the quiet of the library.

Rooms: 26: 1 S, 23 D, 2 Ste, all en suite.
Price: S L180,000-240,000; D L230,000-360,000; Ste L320,000-400,000.
Breakfast: Included.
Meals: Lunch/ Dinner Il Pavone restaurant, choice of set menu or à la carte.
Closed: Never.

How to get there: From E45 Perugia-Terni exit at Ripabianca and follow sign towards Canalicchio.

Hotel Le Silve
Loc. Armenzano
06081 Assisi PG

Tel: 075 801 9000
Fax: 075 801 9005
E-mail: hotellesilve@tin.it
web: www.lesilve.it

Sig.ra Daniela Taddia

The bread is home-made, the cheese and milk are fresh, the hams and salami look worth fighting over. What's more, all of these delicious things are organic, too. The setting, in the heart of the Umbrian hills, provides the sort of snapshot memories that will keep you going through a long, cold winter at home. It is remote (do make sure that you fill up with petrol before leaving Spello or Assisi), but most visitors will revel in that; those who don't will be kept happy by an unexpected range of 'facilities'. The swimming pool has a bar, and there even is hydromassage for the sybaritic among you, with a sauna in which to unwind. You'll find a tennis court, too, plus table-tennis — and hectares of hills and woods in which to ride or walk. The atmosphere is as warm and friendly as you could wish and all ages will find something to amuse them; this is certainly one of those places where you feel happy doing 'your own thing'. Life here started in the 10th century, and continues as a mix of farming and tourism. The bedrooms have stone walls, beautiful furniture and a confident sense of smart simplicity.

Rooms: 15 D, all en suite.
Price: L150,000 p.p. Half-board:
L190,000 p.p. Full-board: L220,000 p.p.
Breakfast: Included.
Meals: Lunch/Dinner on request
L40,000.
Closed: November-March.

How to get there: From Assisi continue up hill circling town, pass under city gate leaving the city. Follow road to right turn for Armenzano. Follow the signs to Le Silve for about 12km of winding country road.

Map Ref No: 11

Brigolante

Via Costa di Trex. 31
06081 Assisi PG

Tel: 075 802 250
Fax: 075 802 250
E-mail: brigolante@edisons.it

Sig. Ugo Bagnoli

Among the foothills of St. Francis' beloved Mount Subascio, a short distance from Assisi, this 16th-century stone farmhouse has been lovingly restored by Stefano and Rebecca Bagnoli. Rebecca is a native American and originally came over to study — the classic love story; the rest is history. Stefano is an architectural land surveyor so this was the perfect project for the young newly weds. A welcome basket awaits, full of goodies from the farm: wine, eggs, cheese, honey, olive oil and home-made jams. In the bathrooms Rebecca leaves her handmade soap and a little sprig of lavender. There are pigs on the farm, so they also produce ham, salami and sausages, as well as red and white wine. From the vegetable garden you may pick whatever you like, eg red peppers, fat tomatoes and huge lettuces. The rooms are light and airy and much of Stefano's grandmother's furniture has been used. The apartments are quite independent but guests can come together in the evening in the communal garden. You are deep in the Mount Subasio National Park so you may prefer just to wander off; dozens of trails await.

Rooms: 3 Apt for 2-4.
Price: L90,000 per day. L500,000 per week.
Breakfast: Self-catering.
Meals: Self-catering.
Closed: Never.

How to get there: Take Assisi ring road following to Porta Perlici and continue towards Gualdo Tadino for 6km. Turn right on the gravel road marked by a signpost for Polombara. Over the first bridge and right, over the second very narrow bridge. Continue up hill for about 500m, turn right at first gravel road.

Hotel Palazzo 'Bocci'

Via Cavour 17
06038 Spello PG

Tel: 0742 301 021
Fax: 0742 301 464
E-mail: bocci@bcsnet.it
web: www.emmeti.it/p.bocci.it.html

Sig. Fabrizio Buono

A beautiful town house right in the centre of Spello opposite S. Andrea church. The pale yellow façade with dove grey shutters and a tiny wooden door within a door does little to announce such a grand interior. The soothing trickle of water from a tiny fountain greets you as you enter the small courtyard which leads to a series of gloriously fine reception rooms. Many have painted friezes but the most impressive is the richly-decorated drawing room know as the *sala degli affreschi* which depicts mercantile scenes. There is also a reading room filled with old books and travel magazines. The bedrooms are a little simpler; most have plain white walls and chestnut beamed ceilings. Breakfast is served in one of the special sitting rooms or on the terrace in warmer weather. A herringbone tiled terrace overlooks the ancient terracotta tiled rooftops of the town and is a perfect place for pre-prandial drinks. You cross the street to the restaurant Il Molino; it was once the village oil mill and here you can dine under the brick vaulted ceiling, a delightful bit of engineering.

Rooms: 23: 2 S, 15 D, 6 Ste (for 4), all en suite.
Price: S L110-140,000; D L200-250,000; Ste L300-350,000.
Breakfast: Included.
Meals: At restaurant 'Il Molino' approx. L50,000.
Closed: Never.

How to get there: From Assisi follow signs towards Spello and Foligno after 10km exit the main road at Spello. In the centre of Spello, hotel opposite Church of S. Andrea

Map Ref No: 11

Marches/Lazio

"Nobody in Rome works and if it rains in Rome and they happen to notice it they blame it on Milan. In Rome people spend most of their time having lunch. And they do it very well - Rome is unquestionably the lunch capital of the world."

Fran Lebowitz

La Lama
Strada Pugliano 4
61018 San Leo PS

Tel: 0541 926 928
E-mail: lalama@tin.it

Conte Ulisse Nardini

Dogs, cats and ducks welcome you as effusively as does the Count Ulisse Nardini himself. He's a colourful character with a ready smile, a very modern scion of a very ancient family who has added a very personal and distinguished touch to this lovely old place. The bedrooms are exquisitely simple with, for example, modern wrought-iron bedsteads, painted headboards, beamed ceilings, pretty floral curtains, well-framed prints, crisply functional but attractive furniture and plain colours on the beds. It is too stylish and pretty to be called 'traditional' and it is all enormously comfortable. The food is a big feature, all of it from ingredients that are natural, regional and produced by the local 'artisans'. There is a happy fusion here of the gastronomic cultures of Romagna, Tuscany and the Marches. Wines are at the top of the heap, with passion brought to bear on the selection of the best available locally. It will be hard not to overdo the eating. The house stands rather engagingly under the rocky pinnacle of San Leo, a splendid, impressive medieval fort and a gem in itself.

Rooms: 7: 1 Tw and 1 D, sharing bathroom, 2 D and 3 Tr all with private bathrooms.
Price: L80,000 for shared bathroom, L100,000 en suite.
Breakfast: Included.
Meals: Dinner L35,000.
Closed: Never.

How to get there: Take SS258 from Rimini for Novafeltria. At Villanuova turn left for San Leo. In village turn left just before the castle, continue for 5km and turn right for La Lama.

108

Map Ref No: 9

Casa Laura
Loc. Montescatto 12
61045 Cagli PS

Tel: 0721 799 275

Sig.ra Laura Radice

The journey from Tuscany to the Marches is one of gentle change, from dry, olive-tree speckled, rolling hills to sharper inclines and forests and then to the relatively untouched, rougher-edged beauty of the Marches. Casa Laura is a small, organic farm, almost totally self-sufficient and thus already appealing to many travellers tired of a supermarket-led existence at home. Breakfasts are home-made feasts, as honest as they are delicious, and you should try the dinners, too. Laura cooks with as much pleasure and humour as she applies to including you in her life. The bedrooms are delightfully basic, without frills and flimflam: wrought-iron bedheads, old country furniture and geometric tiled floors... perfect for the summer heat. The family room downstairs is yours, too, informal and easy with the delightful smell of woodsmoke. This is a wonderful launching pad for long walks in the Appenines, there are distant mountain views, river-swimming for the brave-hearted, and the Adriatic is only 30 minutes away. But do remember that it is basic, ideal for walkers rather than Sybarites, and for those who enjoy a bit of banter in Italian.

Rooms: 4 D, all en suite.
Price: L40,000 p.p. Children half-price.
Breakfast: Included.
Meals: Lunch and dinner on request.
Closed: January.

How to get there: Exit SS3 Roma/Fano at Aqualunga and follow the road (SP111) uphill towards Tarugo. After about 11km turn left at the signpost for Casa Laura.

Map Ref No: 9

Locanda San Rocco

Fraz. Collaiello 2
62020 Gagliole MC

Tel: 0737 641 900
Fax: 0737 642 324

Sig.ra Gisla Pirri

'Solid' is the word. It is all utterly decent, honest taste without a whiff of pretension or a trace of 'naff' modern corner-cutting. It calls itself, rather engagingly, a 'touristic farmhouse' — which I suppose it is. 18th-century, with its old brick walls and ceiling beams suitably exposed in the public rooms, it has kept a purity of style and a sense of great space downstairs, with sweeping expanses of quarry tiles. The bedrooms are attractively plain and simple, with that attractive brickwork above the beams that is so common in Italy. The beds may be of wrought-iron or handsome wood, the furniture straightforward and properly old-fashioned, and the walls almost bare, but the overall effect is charming. The house is part of a 55 hectare estate which supplies the inn with fresh vegetables and fruit the whole year round as well as wine, olive oil, cheese and free-range poultry. The countryside is wooded and rolling, lusher than Tuscany's and in an area little spoiled. The inn can let you have mountain bikes for exploring, a great liberator. There is stacks to do and see locally, so do give this area a try.

Rooms: 6 D, all en suite.
Price: D L120,000.
Breakfast: Included.
Meals: À la carte.
Closed: November — April.

How to get there: From SS361 turn left approx. 1km after Castelraimondo (heading towards S. Severino Marche) for Gagliole. From Gagliole follow indications to Collaiello and La Locanda.

Map Ref No: 12

Squelchia Botta

Maccina Rota
00001 Olivera

E-mail: squebo@porco-online.org
web: www.porco-online.org/squelchiarama.htm

Sig.ra Fango Porco

OK, so the company is not what you might have chosen, but when you are going on holiday you have to take with you a rare flexibility and willingness to go with the flow... In this case you will be sorely challenged, admittedly, but there is good swill in abundance. If you have ever shared a room in a youth hostel, say, you will cope with the nocturnal grunting, the snuffling, the roaming about looking for water in the night, the frequent visits to the loo, even the unexpected snuggles from an unwanted neighbour. It will help you to remember Winston Churchill's comment: "Odd things, animals. Dogs look up to you. Cats look down to you. Only a pig looks at you as an equal." The floor-covering is a genuine weakness here, so take a pallet to provide a bit of height. Gorgeous countryside just a few feet away, with rocky outcrops and old olive trees two a penny. The annexe, engagingly raised on four wheels, is spartan and challenging, but then so is the whole experience. It has certainly encouraged the recent drift to towns that has so denuded Italy's rural areas of people.

Rooms: 1 Car Interior, slightly soiled.
Price: Free to those who can afford it.
Breakfast: Olives available, plus Parma Ham if you bring a utensil.
Meals: Pizza delivery available (see directions).
Closed: Never, due to insecure fittings.

How to get there: Left at The Trough (a local eatery of some reknown) and then listen...

Casa Giardino
Via Adamello 6
00141 Rome RM

Tel: 06 871 82 503

Sig.ra Vanna Vanni

From Rome's hubbub and frenzy to this secluded oasis is but a step. It is in the heart of the Monte Sacro district, in a quiet residential area, close enough to the centre to make you feel part of the Roman experience but far enough to allow you to feel free from entrapment. The house was built at the beginning of the century so has an easier time staying spotlessly clean than its many older colleagues. The garden is a place to while away the morning after a Roman binge. Your hosts, who run the place themselves, are absolutely delightful; they are open, genuine, cultured and knowledgeable. Vanna is an artist so the easy good taste of the house is not a surprise. There are two apartments, each for up to four people. Walls are white, some furniture is decorated; the overall atmosphere is of simplicity, light and space, yet homely too. The rooms are a bit small but with personal flourishes that make them work well, and a lightly formal touch. Rome is a demanding city, and this is a great place to rediscover your own rhythm.

Rooms: 2 Apt: for 2-4.
Price: L800,000 + L25,000 linens weekly.
Breakfast: Self-catering.
Meals: Self-catering.
Closed: Never.

How to get there: From the city ring road exit at Via Nomentana and head towards the centre. Once you arrive in Piazza Sempione, turn into Via Gargano. On to Via Adriatico, turn left off Piazzale Adriatico, after 100m left into Via Stelvio. On to Piazza Elba and Via Adamello is off the Piazza.

Map Ref No: 11

Vicolo della Penitenza 19
00165 Rome RM

Tel: 0335 620 5768
Fax: 06 697 870 84
E-mail: info@insiemesalute.it

Sig.ra Marta Nicolini

If you are feeling a little adventurous and are lucky enough to be planning more than a fleeting trip to Rome, Vicolo della Penitenza is a great little base for you, deep in the fascinating old quarter of Trastevere and an easy walk from St. Peters. The area, though residential, has a lively atmosphere and it's fun to feel more than a mere tourist as you shop for groceries or stop for a drink in the local bar before returning to your little cobbled street. Signora Nicolini has furnished the sunny first floor two bedroom apartment as if it were her own home. She has kept the original brown and black tiled paving but has, overall, added a more contemporary look to this 19th-century town house. There is plenty of room, with an open-plan living room and screened kitchen, white sofas, a good collection of prints, kilim rugs and antique pieces. The queen-size double bedroom is especially inviting, with a beautiful hand-quilted and embroidered bedspread. It is good to come 'home' and put your feet up after a long day.

Rooms: 1 Apt: for 2-4.
Price: L200,000-400,000, minimum 4 days.
Breakfast: Self-catering.
Meals: Self-catering.
Closed: Never.

How to get there: From Ponte Sisto cross Piazza Trilussa and turn right into Via della Lungara. Right into Via dei Riari and first right again into Vicolo della Penitenza 19.

Map Ref No: 11

Villa del Parco

Via Nomentana 110
00161 Rome RM

Tel: 06 442 37 773
Fax: 06 442 37 572
E-mail: villaparco@mclink.it
web: www.venere.it/roma/villaparco

Sig.ra Elisabetta Bernardini

The frenzy of Rome can wear down even the most enthusiastic of explorers, so here is another quiet, dignified, place to which you can retreat and recover your sense of self. There is certainly enough greeness to refresh you — the house is surrounded by trees and shrubs and has a seductive-looking terrace to which you can repair with your book, or a drink. The road is a comforting 30 yards away and from the back of the house at least can hardly be heard. Inside, the mood is refined, elegant, courteous — the house has been run as a hotel by the family for 40 years. There is a hint of Laura Ashley in the bedrooms, reproduction antiques and modern comforts at your elbow, and enough plain colours to ward off a hotel atmosphere. The rooms are a decent size, with fitted carpets that have not undermined the slightly old-fashioned feel. The remnants of frescoes on the staircase are a comforting reminder that you are firmly in Italy, though the house is turn-of-the-century. It is solid and reliable; nothing exotic or eyebrow-raising, but you can hardly fail to be comfortable, particularly as your hosts are as pleasant as their villa.

Rooms: 30: 14 S, 10 D, 6 Tr, all en suite.
Price: S L215,000; D L275,000;
Tr L315,000.
Breakfast: Included.
Meals: Not available.
Closed: Never.

How to get there: From Termini train station turn right into Via XX Settembre and proceed straight past Piazza di Porta Pia into Via Nomentana.

114

Hotel Villa delle Rose

Via Vicenza 5
00185 Rome RM

Tel: 06 445 1788
Fax: 06 445 1639
E-mail: villadellerose@flashnet.it

Sig. Claude Frank

For some reason accommodation near city train stations always seem to conjure up a bad image, noise, commotion and who know what else? But Villa delle Rose though just around the corner from Rome's central station, Termini, is just the opposite and provides a safe haven. A 19th-century villa which once belonged to Roman nobility, the house is set back in it's own grounds with a pleasant garden and terrace on a quiet side street. Claude is Swiss but has lived in Italy for over 20 years and runs the hotel with his Italian wife and family. The whole place has an amiable feeling of fading grandeur with a large, quite grand lounge with faux marble columns and painted ceiling. Oriental rugs are scattered here and there. The rooms are traditionally decorated with floral wall paper and prints. They vary in size from simple doubles to a larger split level quad with balustrated balcony, many have high stuccoed ceilings, some of the rooms look out onto the garden, all are light and airy with large period windows. The Franks are open and sociable hosts ready to welcome you and help in whatever way they may.

Rooms: 37: 8 S, 29 D/Tw 1Q,
all en suite.
Price: S L120,000-200,000;
D L180,000-300,000, L250,000-300,000.
Breakfast: Included.
Meals: Not available.
Closed: Never.

How to get there: From Termini Station enter Via Masala, Via Vicenza is behind Sacra Cuore church.

Map Ref No: 11

115

B&B Vatican Museums

Via Sebastiano Veniero 78
00192 Rome RM

Tel: 06 682 10776
Fax: 06 682 15921
E-mail: bbcenter@tin.it
web: www.bbroma.com/vening.htm

Sig.ra Erminia Pascucci

Just three minutes walk form the Vatican... hence the name! The B&B Vatican Museums makes a relaxing change from staying in a hotel and is perfect for families. It is a large apartment in a turn-of-the-century russet-coloured town house just off a busy road but approached through an attractive communal courtyard dominated by a fine palm tree. This is a real home from home, unpretentious and informal. Erminea is friendly, easy going and speaks English well; she is a graphic artist and out most of the day but gives you the run of the kitchen leaving cereals, bread, pastries and jams for you to help yourself. The three bedrooms are simple but attractive with brightly coloured bedspreads, white-washed walls with framed posters and marbled tiled floors. There are overhead ceiling fans too — a boon when it's hot. The views are not particularly exciting but no matter; there is so much to see in Rome.

Rooms: 3: 1 Tw, 2 D, sharing bathroom, 1 D en suite bath.
Price: D/Tw from L120,000-150,000.
Breakfast: Included.
Meals: Not available.
Closed: Never.

How to get there: From circular road take Via Aurelia following indication for Citta del Vaticano. On Via Candia turn right into Via Sebastiano Veniero

Map Ref No: 11

Aventino Sant' Anselmo

Piazza Sant'Anselmo 2
00153 Rome RM

Tel: 06 574 5231/5174/5232/3547
Fax: 06 578 3604
web: www.aventinohotels.com

Sig.ra Roberta Piroli

You really can walk anywhere in Rome from the Sant' Anselmo: the Colosseum is a couple of minutes away. The hotel was originally four houses and each room is different. Many are in muted yellows and greys with fresco-like stencils: a touch over the top for some, but well done. Some rooms are small, although even the singles have queen-size beds. The best are at the top, up three floors with no lift, but it's worth it. Two of these rooms have terraces but even from the others you look out on the whole of Rome. Bathrooms vary a lot, from large with hydro-massage baths to shower rooms with no window. The hotel has a shady ground-level terrace and a garden, with tables and chairs under a pergola — a great place for a drink after all that walking. Signora Pirolla may seem a bit aloof, an effect which is reinforced by her immaculate appearance, but she will make you feel at home among the antiques and rather ornate décor. Breakfast is served in the bar or on the terrace, or in your room if you like. You can park in the courtyard if you came by car... a huge bonus in Rome.

Rooms: 50: 11 S, 32 D, 7 Tr/Q,
all en suite.
Price: S L210,000; D L320,000;
Tr L370,000; Q L400,000.
Breakfast: Included.
Meals: Restaurants nearby.
Closed: Never.

How to get there: Opposite 'ostienze' (train station) cross the piazza, keeping it on your left, on reaching another small square with 4 roads branching off it, take the second one on your right. This is Via Aventino; the hotel is on your left at a junction with another road comming from your direction.

Self-catering
These places have only self-catering accommodation.

Piedmont
4

Veneto
28

Liguria
38

Tuscany
63 • 66 • 74 • 78 • 81 • 82 • 83 • 93

Umbria
97 • 98 • 101 • 106

Lazio
112 • 113

Self-catering and B&B
These places have B&B and self-catering accommodation.

Piedmont
3 • 5 • 10

Lombardy
20 • 21 • 22

Liguria
40 • 41 • 42 • 49 • 51 • 55 • 56

Tuscany
61 • 65 • 67 • 69 • 72 • 79 • 84 • 85 • 87 • 94

Umbria
99

Good for singles
These places have single rooms or do not charge single supplements.

Piedmont
1 • 2 • 4 • 6

Lombardy
12 • 13 • 16 • 18 • 21 • 22 • 24 • 25

Trentino-Alto
26

Veneto
27

Liguria
41 • 45 • 47 • 50 • 52 • 53 • 54

Tuscany
59 • 60 • 61 • 64 • 67 • 70 • 71 • 76 • 77 • 80 85 • 88 • 90 • 92

Umbria
100 • 103 • 104 • 107

Lazio
114 • 115 • 117

Organic
Owners of these places tell us they use organic or home-grown produce cultivated without chemicals.

Piedmont
1 • 2 • 4 • 8 • 9 • 10

Lombardy
18

Liguria
36 • 38 • 39 • 42 • 43 • 44 • 48 • 49 • 51 • 56 57 • 58

Tuscany
59 • 60 • 69 • 70 • 72 • 76

Umbria
101 • 102 • 105

Vegetarians catered for
Owners of these places provide vegetarian food. Please let them know your requirements in advance..

Piedmont
1 • 2 • 3 • 4 • 5 • 8 • 9

Lombardy
15 • 18 • 24

Emilia Romagna
29

Liguria
36 • 39 • 42 • 43 • 44
• 45 • 47 • 48 • 49 • 52
53 • 56 • 57 • 58

Tuscany
59 • 61 • 62 • 64 • 65
• 68 • 69 • 70 • 72 • 76
80 • 84 • 90 • 91 • 96
• 101 • 102 • 103

Wheelchair
Owners of these places tell us they
have facilities suitable for people in
wheelchairs. Confirm availabillity
when booking.

Piedmont
4 • 9

Lombardy
20 • 21

Emilia Romagna
29 • 32

Liguria
45 • 50

Tuscany
64 • 68 • 70 • 81 • 89
• 96 • 104 • 106 • 107
114 • 117

Bike
You can either borrow or hire bikes
at these places.

Piedmont
1 • 2 • 4 • 6 • 7 • 8
• 10

Lombardy
18 • 20 • 21

Emilia Romagna
29 • 36 • 38 • 39 • 40
• 42 • 43 • 44 • 45 • 48

49 • 56 • 60 • 61 • 63
• 65 • 67 • 69 • 78 • 80
81 • 82 • 83 • 91 • 102
• 104 • 110

Wine
These places have vineyards and
make their own wine.

Piedmont
5 • 6 • 7 • 8

Lombardy
19

Veneto
28

Emilia-Romagna
35

Liguria
38 • 39 • 43 • 51 • 56
58

Tuscany
66 • 72 • 78 • 90

Umbria
102

Marches
110

Olive oil
These places produce their own
olive oil.

Emilia Romagna
35

Liguria
39 • 51 • 56 • 58

Tuscany
65 • 66 • 72 • 78 • 81
• 90

Umbria
96 • 102 • 106

Lazio
110

Making the booking

Good morning/afternoon-evening	*Buongiorno/Buonasera*
Do you speak English?	*Parla inglese?*
Do you have a	*Avete disponibile una camera*
single	*singola*
double	*matrimoniale*
twin	*doppia*
triple room available?	*tripla?*
For this evening/tomorrow	*Per questa sera/domani sera*
Double/twin bed(s)	*Matrimoniale/doppia*
With private bathroom	*Con bagno privato*
Shower/bathtub	*Doccia/vasca*
Balcony	*Terrazza*
Is breakfast included?	*E compresa la colazione?*
Half-board	*Mezza pensione*
Full board	*Mezza pensione completa*
How much does it cost?	*Quanto costa?*
May we bring our pet monkey?	*Possiamo portare la nostra scimmia?*
We will arrive at 6 pm	*Arriviamo alle sei*
We would like to have dinner	*Desideriamo fare la cena*

Getting there

Left/right	*Sinistra/destra*
Excuse me	*Mi scusi*
We're lost	*Siamo persi*
Where is...	*Dove...*
Could you show us on the map where we are?	*Mi puo indicare sulla cartina dove siamo?*
We are in Rosia	*Siamo a Rosia*
We will be late	*Arriviamo in ritardo*
Could you send a tractor to pull us out of the ditch please?	*Potete demandarci un trattore da tirarci fuori del fosso per favore?*

On arrival

Hello	*Salve*
We have a booking in the. name of...	*Abbiamo una prenotazione nel nome di...*
We found your name in this guide book	*Abbiamo trovato la vostra struttura in questa guida*
Where can we leave the car?	*Dove possiamo parcheggiare l'auto?*
May I see a room?	*Posso vedere una camera?*
I would like to book a room	*Vorrei prenotare una camera*
We will stay 3 nights	*Rimaniamo tre notti*

While you are there

Do you have an extra pillow/blanket?	*Ha un cuscino/una coperta in piu?*
A light bulb needs replacing	*Una lampadina e fulminata*
We have left the key in the room	*Abbiamo lasciato le chiavi in camera*
The room is too cold/too hot	*La camera e troppo fredda/calda*
Do you have a fan?	*Ha un ventilatore?*
The heating/air-conditioning doesn't work	*Il riscaldamento/condizionatore d'aria non funzione*
There is no hot water	*Non c'e acqua calda*
The room's too quiet, we can't sleep!	*La camera e troppo silenzioso, non si riesce a dormire!*
Could someone come and help me please	*Qualcuno puo venire ad aiutarmi per favore?*
What time is breakfast?	*A che ora c'è la colazione?*
lunch?	*pranzo?*
dinner?	*cena?*

On leaving

What time is check out?	*A che ora dobbiamo lasciare l'appartamento?*
We would like to pay the bill	*Vogliamo pagare il conto*
Do you take credit cards?	*Accetta la carta di credito?*
Are you looking for a new employee by any chance?	*Cercate un nuovo impiegato per caso?*
Bye Bye!	*Arrivederci!*

On salivating

Acciughe or Alici	Anchovies
Agnello	Lamb
Anatra	Duck
Animelle	Sweetbreads
Aragosta	Lobster
Aringhe	Herrings
Carne di castrato/suino	Mutton/Pork
Cervo	Venison
Coniglio	Rabbit
Cozze	Mussels
Granchio	Crab
Lumache	Snails
Manzo	Beef
Merluzzo	Cod
Ostriche	Oysters
Pollo	Chicken
Tacchino	Turkey
Vitello	Veal

Alastair Sawday's
Special Places to Stay

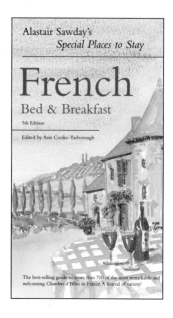

French Bed & Breakfast

Don't plan a trip to France without this book!

It has become a much-loved travelling companion for many thousands of visitors to France. What a treat it is to travel knowing that someone else whom you can trust has done the researching, agonising and diplomatic work for you already. Wherever you are there will be, not too far away, a warm welcome from a French (or English) family keen to draw you into their home and give you a slice of French hospitality.

The selection has been honed over 5 editions, and is delectable. We can almost guarantee you a good time! And you will, too, save a small fortune on hotel prices.

One reader wrote to tell us that we had changed her life! Well, we don't claim to do that, but it does seem that we have changed the way thousands of people travel.

Price: £13.95

Alastair Sawday's
Special Places to Stay

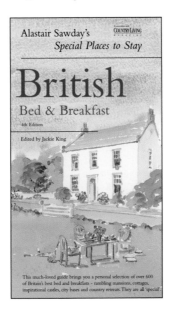

British Bed & Breakfast

A delightful selection of B&Bs to inspire you to get away - to the hills, the sea, to deepest countryside, to exciting cities. There are exquisite cottages, majestic castles, lochside retreats, woodland hideaways, an Augustinian monastery and an old Trinity House signal station.

Our hosts will introduce you to their beloved corner of Britain, invite you to share their homes and do their all to make sure your stay is special. Exquisite dinners or simple suppers are available in many of our houses - most meals are excellent value and many of our hosts use locally-produced and organic food, too.

With an easy-to-use map, excellent directions and a section listing a county-by-county guide to houses especially suitable for those wanting to eat organically, for singles, for wheelchair users and those travelling with children or pets.

Can you think of exploring Britain without this book?

Price: £12.95

Alastair Sawday's
Special Places to Stay

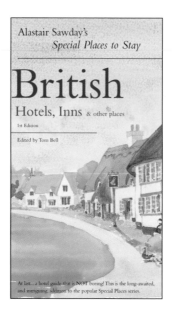

Alastair Sawday's
Special Places to Stay

British

Hotels, Inns & other places

1st Edition

Edited by Tom Bell

At last... a hotel guide that is NOT boring! This is the long-awaited, and intriguing addition to the popular Special Places series.

British Hotels, Inns and other places

Are British Hotels as bad as we think? Have any survived the onslaught of mass tourism and the corporate culture of our age? Where are they?

Come and meet them! This book is a triumph: we knew enough good hotels, inns and other places to be sure that there were others. We have found them, and this book celebrates them - and all those owners who have persisted in doing their own thing, and doing it brilliantly.

If you prefer the unexpected to the predictable; if you prefer home-made food to the pre-packaged suff; if you would rather a day on a mountain than one in a theme park; if you would rather be served by a human being with some personality than by a 'hospitality executive'... then this book is for you.

Price: £10.95

Alastair Sawday's
Special Places to Stay

Spain & Portugal

This unusual book has given terrific pleasure to readers, galvanising many into wider-ranging exploration of the hinterland of Spain and Portugal. Almost everywhere people have met with a warm reception, wonderful people and their fascinating houses and hotels.

The third edition has a richer and more eclectic selection than ever, an irresible gathering of the curious, the beautiful and the very comfortable. There are the usual grand country houses, the inevitable ancient palaces, predictably comely religious buildings and reliable old farmhouses. But now add stone-carved town mansions, sprawling ranches, mills, old *bodegas*, mountain retreats and seaside villas. Here is a cornucopia of delights, a panoply of pleasures, selected because they are fun, alive, warm and human.

How to spend a holiday in Spain and Portugal without ever wasting a night? And without spending a fortune? Here is the answer.

Price: £11.95

Alastair Sawday's
Special Places to Stay

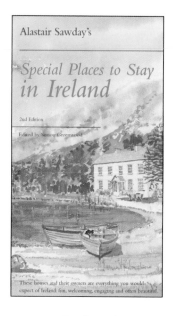

Alastair Sawday's

Special Places to Stay
in Ireland

2nd Edition

Edited by Simon Greenwood

These houses and their owners are everything you would expect of Ireland: fun, welcoming, engaging and often beautiful.

Ireland

The editor himself says "This is a corker of a book!" Indeed, it is. There is nothing quite like it on the subject of sleeping and carousing in Ireland. If you ever doubted for one moment that the Irish are the most entertaining and sumptuously alive people in Europe, then Special Places will put you right.

But that is not all, of course. The houses and hotels in this book are an architectural feast, a riot of colour and variety, of unexpected comforts and surprising touches of personality.

"... a superb book..., and it's honest-to-goodness, top notch. It's only £10.95 and worth at least double that."

John Clayton's 'Travel with a Difference'

This is the second edition of this much-loved and trusted book.

Price: £10.95

Alastair Sawday's
Special Places to Stay

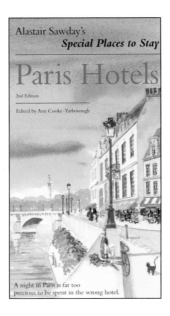

Paris Hotels

Things change so quickly... how on earth are you to know which hotels are still attractive and good value? Which *quartiers* are still liveable and quiet? Where has the long arm of the corporate hotel world NOT reached?

Well, you are lucky to hear of this book... it will rescue your weekend! This second edition follows a successful first edition, still with just a small, select number of our very favourite hotels.

Ann Cooke-Yarborough has lived in Paris for years and has tramped the streets to research and upgrade this second edition. She has chosen with an eagle eye for humbug. Unerringly, she has selected the most interesting, welcoming, good-value hotels in Paris, leaving out the pompous, the puffed-up, the charmless and the ugly.

Trust our taste and judgement, and enjoy some good descriptive writing. With the colour photos, the symbols and the light touch, you have a gem of a book.

Price: £10.95

Alastair Sawday's
'Special Places' Walks

Our *walks* are as unusual, different and imaginative as our *books*... and based on the same conviction that people matter as much as places.

If you enjoy walking rather than hiking, if you would like to be guided by an English-speaking local and want to sleep in houses or hotels from *Special Places*, then do join in. We take small groups of 8 to Andalucia, Tuscany and the French Pyrenees.

Our food is terrific, we carry your luggage, we invariably have fun... want to know more?

Get in touch:
0117 929 9921 (Fax: 0117 925 4712)
E-mail: contact@sawdays.co.uk
Internet:www.sawdays.co.uk

Order Form for the UK

See over for USA

All these books are available in the major bookshops but we can send them to you quickly and without effort on your part. Post and packaging is FREE if you order 3 or more books.

	No. of copies	Price each	Total value
British Bed & Breakfast - 4th Edition		£12.95	
British Hotels, Inns and other places		£10.95	
French Bed & Breakfast - 5th Edition		£13.95	
Paris Hotels		£8.95	
Special Places to Stay: Spain & Portugal		£11.95	
Special Places to Stay: Ireland		£10.95	
Special Places to Stay: Italy		£ 9.95	

ADD Post & Packaging: £1 for Paris, Italy or British Hotels books,
£2 for any other, FREE if ordering 3 or more books.

Total Order value

Please make cheques payable to Alastair Sawday Publishing.

All orders to:

Alastair Sawday Publishing, 44 Ambra Vale East, Bristol BS8 4RE.

Name

Address

Postcode

Tel

Fax

For credit card payments please call us on: 0117 929 9921.

We accept Visa, Mastercard, Switch and Solo

Order Form for the USA

These books are available at your local bookstore, or you may order direct. Allow two or three weeks for delivery.

	No. of copies	Price each	Total value
British Bed & Breakfast		$19.95	
British Hotels, Inns and other places		$14.95	
French Bed & Breakfast		$19.95	
Paris Hotels		$14.95	
Special Places to Stay in Spain & Portugal		$19.95	
Special Places to Stay in Ireland		$19.95	

Shipping in the continental USA: $3.95 for one book, $4.95 for two books, $5.95 for three or more books.

Outside continental USA, call (800) 243-0495 for prices. _____

For delivery to AK, CA, CO, FL, GA, IL, IN, KS, MI, MN, MO, NE, NM, NC, OK, SC, TN, TX, VA, and WA, please add the appropriate sales tax. _____

TOTAL ORDER _____

Please make checks payable to: The Globe Pequot Press

To order by phone with Mastercard or Visa: (800) 243-0495, 9am to 5pm EST, by fax: (800) 820-2329, 24 hours; through our Web site: www.globe-pequot.com; or by mail: The Globe Pequot Press, P.O. Box 480, Guilford, CT 06437.

Name _____ Date _____

Address _____

Town _____

State _____ Zip code _____

Tel _____ Fax _____

Report Form

Comments on existing entries and new discoveries.
If you have any comments on entries in this guide, please let us have them.

If you have a favourite house, hotel or inn or a new discovery, please let us know about it.

Report on:

Entry no.

New Recommendation

Date

Name of hotel/B&B

Address

Postcode

Tel:

My reasons are:

continued..

_____

_____

_____

_____

_____

_____

_____

_____

_____

_____

_____

_____

_____

_____

My name and address:
_____

Name
_____

Address
_____

Postcode
_____

Tel (only if you don't mind)
_____

Please send the completed form to:

Alastair Sawday Publishing, 44 Ambra Vale East, Bristol BS8 4RE, UK

Thank you so much for your help!

Reservation Form

Attenzione di all: To: _____

Da parte di: From: _____

Nome della struttura ricettiva: Name of property: _____

_____

Gentili Signori, Dear Sirs,

Ho (abbiamo) visto la Vs. struttura sulla guida Alastair Sawday's Special Places to Stay in Italy e pertanto vorrei (vorremmo) prenotare in nome di
We have seen your property in the guide book Alastair Sawday's Special Places to Stay in Italy and would like to make a reservation in the name of

_____

_____

Per	*notte(i)*	*Arrivo:*	*giorno*	*mese*	*anno*
For	night(s)	Arriving:	day	month	year
		Partenza:	*giorno*	*mese*	*anno*
		Leaving:	day	month	year

Si richiede n. sistemazione(i) in:
We require a total of _____ room as follows: _____

Singola n.	*con bagno*	*Doppia n.*	*con bagno*
Single (no.) with bathroom		Double (no.) with bathroom	
Tripla n.	*con bagno*	*Quadrupla n.*	*con bagno*
Triple (no.) with bathroom		Quadruple (no.) with bathroom	
Suite n.	*con bagno*	*Appartamento n.*	*per n.* *persone*
Suite (no.) with bathroom		Apartment for	persons

Si richiede anche la somministrazione della cena per n. persona(e)
We will also be requiring dinner for _____ person(s).

Prego inviarmi(ci) una conferma scritta della mia/nostra prenotazione al seguente indirizzo: Please send written confirmation to the address below:

Nome: Name: _____

Indirrizzo: Address: _____

_____

_____

FAX/email: _____

Vi ringrazio per la vostra disponibilita e nell'occassione porgo (porgiamo) distinti saluti. We thank you for your kind attention.

INDEX OF NAMES

INDEX OF PLACES

Exchange rate table......

Italian Lire	Euro	£Sterling
10,000	5.16	3.24
15,000	7.75	4.86
20,000	10.33	6.48
25,000	12.91	8.10
30,000	15.49	9.72
35,000	18.08	11.34
40,000	20.66	12.97
45,000	23.24	14.59
50,000	25.82	16.21
55,000	28.31	17.83
60,000	30.99	19.45
65,000	33.57	21.07
70,000	36.15	22.69
75,000	38.73	24.31
80,000	41.32	25.93
85,000	43.90	27.55
90,000	46.48	29.17
95,000	49.06	30.79
100,000	52.00	32.00
200,000	103.00	65.00
400,000	207.00	130.00
500,000	258.00	162.00
700,000	362.00	227.00
900,000	465.00	292.00
1,000,000	516.00	324.00